Anthony G. Reddie is Director of t
and Culture, Regent's Park College,
an Extraordinary Professor of Theo
of South Africa. His most recent book is *Theologizing Brexit: A Liberationist and Postcolonial Critique* (Routledge, 2019). In June 2020 he received the Lanfranc Award for Outstanding Contribution to Education and Scholarship from the Archbishop of Canterbury.

IS GOD COLOUR-BLIND?

Insights from Black theology for Christian faith and ministry

ANTHONY G. REDDIE

First published in Great Britain in 2009

Society for Promoting Christian Knowledge
36 Causton Street
London SW1P 4ST

Second edition 2020

British Library Cataloguing-in-Publication Data
A catalogue record for this book is available from the British Library

ISBN 978–0–281–08523–1
eBook ISBN 978–0–281–08543–9

Typeset by Fakenham Prepress Solutions, Fakenham, Norfolk NR21 8NL
First printed in Great Britain by MPG
This edition printed by Ashford Colour Press
Subsequently digitally printed in Great Britain

Produced on paper from sustainable forests

To all those who have helped me realize God is not colour-blind – God affirms Blackness. Thank you

Contents

Acknowledgements

My initial thanks are reserved for the many ordinary Black people of faith who worked alongside me in 'road-testing' some of the Black theology ideas in this book. Without you I could never be.

I am thrilled to have been appointed Director of the Oxford Centre for Religion and Culture. Since commencing this role, I have enjoyed the fellowship and collegiality of Regent's Park College, a permanent private hall of the University of Oxford. I have loved the intellectual stimulation of colleagues at the college and the wider context of Oxford, and I offer this book as a modest contribution to the quest for a more diverse and inclusive world of scholarship.

In addition, my thanks go to my good friend, colleague and confidante, Carol Troupe, whose wise counsel over the years has kept me focused and on track.

I would like to thank my family, particularly my deceased mother, Lucille Reddie, who has always been my inspiration. Thanks also to my father, Noel Reddie, but not forgetting my siblings, Richard, Christopher and Sandra, plus my deceased Uncle Mervin and his widow, my Auntie Lynette, and best of all, my nephew Noah and niece Sasha; the next generation of my family. You are all special people in my life, and without you I would be a lesser human being.

Finally, of course, there is God, through whom all things are possible; often making a way out of no way. My gratitude knows no bounds and cannot be expressed in words.

Thank you all.

Introduction

Black theology has been an area of academic study for more than 40 years but it has not very often made its way out of the library and into the world. Yet it can and should be a powerful resource for assisting the Church in fighting racism and recognizing racial justice as the bedrock of the community of faith.

My aim in this book is to provide a resource for ministers, local preachers, lay readers and many others who are engaged in some form of leadership role in the Church to exercise their ministry in a manner that is informed by Black theology. The ideas included here for group activities and Bible study, and the examples of how Black theology might influence sermons, will I hope enable and inspire those involved in ministry to raise awareness of issues of racial justice and to bring about social transformation.

Over the years I have come to understand my own scholarly ministry as that of a *participative Black theologian*. In order to explain what I mean by this term it is necessary to understand what is meant by two other terms: Black theology and practical theology.

Black theology

'Black theology' is the specific self-named enterprise of reinterpreting the meaning of God as revealed in Jesus Christ, in light of the very real experiences, largely of struggle, oppression and sheer hardship, of Black people. This approach to engaging with the Christian tradition is not unlike other forms of 'theologies of liberation'[i] in that

---

[i] Theologies of liberation, sometimes called 'liberation theologies' or even 'third-world theologies', is the collective term for a whole branch of largely politically inspired models of talking about God that are committed to the liberation of the poor and the marginalized. These theologies take as their starting point the material or concrete reality of the marginalized and the oppressed in history and not the doctrinal or official teachings of the Church and Christian tradition. (The scope of the differing forms of marginalization and oppression is broad and includes poverty, 'race', gender, sexuality, disability and much else.) They also begin with the historical analysis of people in particular contexts and their accompanying experiences and realities as they seek to relate these factors to their attempt to talk about a God who is real in their everyday lived circumstances. For

its starting point is the reality of being a Black person in a world run by powerful White people for their own benefit. In the case of Black theology, one begins with reflections on Blackness and the Black experience, which are placed alongside an ongoing dialogue with holy Scripture[1] and the resultant traditions that emerge from within Christianity.

For many, the most important person in the development of Black theology has been the African American theologian, James H. Cone. Cone's landmark trilogy of books in the late 1960s and 1970s, *Black Theology and Black Power*,[2] *A Black Theology of Liberation*[3] and *God of the Oppressed*,[4] remain the dominant texts in outlining the importance of understanding the Christian faith from the perspective of disenfranchised and oppressed Black peoples across the world.

Black theology is understood as the deliberate attempt to connect the reality and substance of being Black and the development of ideas surrounding Blackness with one's sacred talk of God and God's relationship with the mass of suffering humanity who might be described as being Black people.

The term Black in the context of Black theology in Britain has a dual meaning. Its dominant meaning refers to people of African descent, who since the late 1960s have adopted 'Black' as a form of description to identify themselves rather than names and terms used by others, such as 'coloured'.[5] The second meaning is political, to speak of a coalition of groups who have come together in order to fight the central and dominating power that is White Euro-American normality.[6] This second meaning does not restrict the term to those who are of African descent or simply refer to skin colour, but rather opens it up to all people who are non-White and who are struggling in solidarity for liberation over and against the forces of White, male-dominated power structures.[7] Black theology argues that the God revealed in Jesus Christ has entered into history and is in actual solidarity with Black people. In fact, one may even argue that God's presence is *actually* revealed in the life experiences and

a useful overview of this branch of theological reflection, see Virginia Fabella and R. S. Sugirtharajah (eds), *Dictionary of Third World Theologies* (Maryknoll: Orbis, 2000), John Parratt (ed.), *An Introduction to Third World Theologies* (Cambridge: Cambridge University Press, 2004 and Marcella Althaus-Reid, Ivan Petrella and Luiz Carlos Susin (eds), *Another Possible World* (London: SCM Press, 2007).

activity of Black people in the world and not simply through the official liturgies, particularly that of Holy Communion or the Eucharist or the Mass.[8]

Many Black theologians have asserted that Jesus is Black. This statement should not be taken, necessarily, to mean simply that Jesus is literally Black (which is not to deny the importance of Jesus actually being understood as being so).[9] What writers such as James Cone,[10] Jacquelyn Grant[11] and Robert Beckford[12] are stating is that God's preferential option is for the empowerment and affirmation of oppressed peoples, the majority of whom are Black. If Black people were enslaved and continue to be oppressed solely on the grounds of the colour of their skin (the mythical 'curse of Ham' – Genesis 9.18–27 – was used to justify the enslavement of Black people), then God in Christ took the form of these exploited people in order to show God's total identification with their plight. In the context of my own work, the term Black refers primarily to people of African Caribbean descent, but it also includes all minority ethnic people who are marginalized within the body politic of postcolonial Britain.[13]

Practical theology

My work as a participative black theologian has been informed by the theological frameworks provided by the wider discipline(s) and practice of what is now termed practical theology. Scholars such as Ballard and Pritchard,[14] Forrester[15] and Graham[16] have theorized around the development of practical theology as a model of reflective activity in which the theologian interrogates the connections between the theory and practice of Christianity in a diverse range of contexts and settings. Practical theology is the overall framework or approach to the Christian faith that uses different models of thinking, such as psychology, counselling, education and sociology, as ways of looking at God's action in the world. One of the central tasks of practical theology is to consider the relationship between how the Church and individual Christians have considered the meaning of faith in light of what individuals and the Church *actually do* in their daily lived attempts to give expression to what they believe.

My own development as a practical theologian comes from within the more specific discipline of Christian education. The term Christian education can be defined and understood in a variety of ways. Jeff Astley, Leslie J. Francis and Colin Crowder provide a helpful starting point for a definition and a rationale, describing it as:

> The phrase [Christian education is] often used quite generally to refer to those processes by which people learn to become Christian and to be more Christian, through learning Christian beliefs, attitudes, values, emotions and dispositions to engage in Christian actions and to be open to Christian experiences.[17]

For those wishing to undertake preliminary studies into the theory and practice of Christian education, I would also recommend Jeff Astley's *The Philosophy of Christian Religious Education*,[18] chapters 1 and 2 of which deal with questions of definition, philosophy and the rationale for Christian education.

Participative Black theology

A participative Black theology is a form of activity-based approach to theological thinking and action that is based on the notion of Christian believers engaging in what I call 'performative action'. Elsewhere, I have described performative action as action that requires that we creatively engage with the 'other' in a specified space (what one might term 'ecclesia' or 'communities of faithful practice'[19]) in which the rules of engagement are constantly being defined and redefined.[20] I want to stress the importance of Black theology that arises from the creative and playful engagement of ordinary people taking part in exercises and drama, in which, through their shared learning and reflection, new insights that relate to Black theology are able to emerge. So the task of doing Black theology is accomplished by participating in collaborative learning and reflective exercises in order to create new experiences that can assist us in the task of expressing faith in light of the needs of those who are marginalized and oppressed. The use of exercises, games and drama is to provide the framework and the setting in which people can be enabled to use their imaginations and then playfully express new thoughts and construct different ways of acting in light of the Christian faith as a means of being 'changed agents' for justice, peace and equity for all peoples. This is essentially an activist form of Black theological practice.

Through my work I have sought to encourage others to become part of the process that helps to create new knowledge about Black theology, in addition to helping them understand this movement as one of radical Christian inspired action for social transformation.[21] In order to provide an embodied reality for the practice of performative action I have just described, I have created a number of experiential exercises in which adult participants can explore the dynamics of encounter and transformation in a personal, collective and corporate sense within safe learning environments. The thrust for this work has emerged from previous pieces of research.[22] So to be clear, this approach to undertaking Black theology in Britain, which is based upon my own idiosyncratic interests in experiential learning and Christian formation, draws upon the central tenets of Black theology as a means of creating new ways of engaging in this discipline and practice.

My work in this area has been somewhat different from that undertaken by the majority of people who might describe themselves as Black theologians, including James Cone. The difference is that I have sought to operate from within the concrete realities of Christian ministry and practice rather than from theorized, intellectual reflections only. Most Black theologians operate as complex thinkers looking at how one can understand the basic ideas of God as a being grounded in the revelation of God's own self-interaction with humankind for the purposes of liberation and freedom.[23] In my own work I have used concrete contexts or situations, like Christian ministry and worship, to provide a means and a model of seeking to practise Black theology in partnership with ordinary people, both Black and White. I seek to develop models of Black theological reflection and learning that encapsulate the central ideas of Black theology within the practical contexts of Christian ministry.

My development as a scholar has been concerned with attempting to combine Christian education with Black theology in order to provide an accessible framework for the radical reinterpretation of the Christian faith for the transformation of ordinary people. Both my scholarly and my practical work have progressed over a number of phases and have, in more recent times, taken on board the practice of 'racism awareness training' within British theological education.

In most of the historic churches in the Protestant tradition in this country, such as the Church of England, the Methodist Church, the Baptist Union and the United Reformed Church, racism awareness training has been an ingredient of theological education for many years. It is now compulsory for all those training for public ministry within the Methodist Church and in many of its ecumenical partners. This training seeks to make students aware of the historical manifestation of the conceptual idea of 'race' and its dangerous offspring, 'racism'. Of course, in strict terms 'race' does not exist (hence my use of inverted commas). Rather, the notion is a set of unproven frameworks for indicating the notion of fixed categories of biological (and hierarchical) differences between differing groups of people, and is an invention, or fiction, of the era of modernism. A number of scholars have demonstrated the specious nature of such discourse and the ways in which it seeks to create untenable and unstable boundaries between groups of humanity. In the words of the annual 'Racial Justice Sunday' packs of resource material produced by the Churches' Commission for Racial Justice (CCRJ), 'There is only one race – that is the human race'.[24]

Black theology and the struggle for racial justice

Racial awareness training has involved me in the task of enabling predominantly White, middle-class, suburban ministry students to reflect upon the ways in which racism has blighted the lives of Black (and White) people, and to see how their practice of ministry can be a positive force in the anti-racist struggle.

Over the time I have been undertaking this work I have developed a method for seeking to assist these students to understand the central tenets of Black theology and, in so doing, to develop forms of anti-racist and anti-oppressive models of Christian ministry. In this work I have challenged them to think about what it means to be White and in what ways Whiteness plays a part in their understanding of themselves.

In my experience White students have quite often struggled to understand the central ideas of Black theology as it applies to themselves as White people. Often, some of these students have sought to keep Black theology at arm's length in order not to be troubled by the challenges posed by this discipline.

When undertaking racism awareness work I have challenged these students to assess in what ways they can become resources for anti-racist struggle.[25] The onus has been less upon the acquisition of abstract knowledge and information for its own sake than on enabling them to process their feelings, in order that they may begin to own and 'climb inside' the experience of racial injustice as opposed to merely discussing it. I also seek to enable students to set action plans on how their own future ministry will seek not only to be aware of the dangers posed by racism but also the ways in which their calling and vocation as ministers can challenge this phenomenon. An example can be shown in the following anecdote.

I often use a very biting three-part DVD produced by the BBC entitled *The History of Racism*.[26] Part 3 of the DVD, which looks at the manifestation of racism from 1865 and the end of legalized slavery in the United States through to the present day, is a helpful means of challenging predominantly White students. In what is a hard-hitting programme, perhaps the most grisly aspect of the documentary is the vivid, dramatic reconstruction of young African boys in the Belgian Congo having their right hands removed with a machete by representatives of King Leopold II in their efforts to get the native Congolese to extract more rubber for their colonial 'masters'. On occasions, as the dramatic images are suffused with the stark narrative of nearly ten million people dying from the forced-labour regime of Leopold, some White students have left the room in tears while others have had to close their eyes in order to keep the images of such brutalities at bay. Clearly, this is arresting material!

In showing the students this DVD it is not my intention to shock for its own sake. Neither do I want merely to implant in the students' minds yet more facts and figures about the brutal workings of racism and its effects on Black peoples. Rather, my intention is to get this sort of material into their emotions and feelings. I want students to reflect on this material and, with my support and encouragement, as we then look at biblical hermeneutics (interpretation) and theological reflection, to see how and in what ways they can operate to challenge the corruptions and the sinful actions of sometimes so-called 'Good Christians' of the past. As the DVD proceeds to demonstrate, one can trace a direct line from the brutal actions of the past to the more subtle forms of racism that continue to plague Black people in the early twenty-first century.[27]

Students are encouraged to think about ways in which they can seek to utilize the central ideas of Black theology in their future ministry in order to become agents for change. How can ordained ministers provide the necessary leadership that will enable churches, through their outreach and social action, in addition to their worship life, to become beacons for the reign or rule of God, in which all persons are treated with dignity and respect?

Black theology as a resource for transformative ministry

In many respects my decision to concentrate on theological education has been a tactical one, namely, the desire to implant into the hearts and minds of impressionable people the possibilities of seeing their ministry as one of change and transformation for all those with whom they come into contact.[28]

This book seeks to build on that work. I have moved the focus from one purely concerned with the teaching and learning of Black theology in ministerial education to one that is concerned with the broader context of Christian ministry for all persons of faith, whether ordained or lay. Christian ministry and worship are the central contexts in which ordinary Christians and ministers can seek to use the insights of Black theology in order to become signs of hope and models of change for the liberation of all people who are presently marginalized and oppressed.

Such a transformative ministry is fuelled, to my mind, by the passionate energy of Black theology that seeks to give expression and commitment to bringing our radical, real selves before God and not the polite conformist versions often demanded by the paternalistic and passionless models bequeathed to us by imperial, mission theology.[29] In this respect, I am clear that God is not colour-blind. God is not blind to the material realities of struggle and marginalization that afflict the bulk of Black peoples across the world.

To follow the framework of Black theology as the key to reinterpreting the meaning of the Christian faith is to commit oneself to a passionate, no-holds-barred decision to follow the way of the radical Christ who stands against all forms of complacency, self-satisfaction, corporate greed and vested self-interest.[30]

It can be argued that in its attempt to offer a radical, politicized agenda for transformative change, Black theology has not always offered sufficient resources for enabling ordinary Christians to see the means by which the prophetic agenda of this movement could be harnessed within the corporate expressions of worship and ministry. In this text, I seek to offer a more accessible, pastoral and ministry-based model of Black theology that attempts to provide radical resources for empowerment and liberative change.

Whether working through exercises that can be used in worship services or Christian fellowship groups, through to Bible studies and theological reflection in sermons, this book seeks to offer resources that will stimulate thinking and provide the emotional and spiritual basis for action and the wider commitment to change that lies at the heart of Black theology. It is concerned with showing how Christian ministers and those involved in various forms of lay ministry can use Black theology to bring about constructive change and transform the thinking and emotional well-being of ordinary Black and White people. The resources offered will enable the Church to anchor its commitment to the liberating gospel of Jesus Christ and help build a world in which racial justice and freedom for all people is a reality. I hope you enjoy reading and using this book.

Part 1

Insights from Black theology for group exercises and Bible study

1

Affirming difference: avoiding colour-blindness

This chapter offers a creative and participative approach to addressing issues of racial justice within the context of adult Christian education and theological education. In the past twenty years that I have worked as a theological educator, I have developed a range of theological resources for addressing various issues in pastoral ministry and Christian discipleship. Since the mid 1990s, I have become a source of specialist theological knowledge and insight, for example in the areas of racial justice, consciousness-raising and Black empowerment, by means of Black theology and Christian education.

One of my primary aims has been to assist in raising the consciousness/awareness and commitment of ministers and lay people to justice issues, and the creation and development of the following exercise has been influenced by such concerns. However, it should not be construed as being a specific or dedicated racial-justice training initiative per se. Rather, this exercise is essentially a contextual and applied theological approach to transforming individuals and churches, and our assumptions about the nature and role of the Christian faith in predominantly Western technological, liberal democratic nations. I am interested in creating learning opportunities for lay and ordained people (principally those who have leadership responsibilities), in order that they may affirm and empower others in the Christian faith.

An exercise in affirming difference

This exercise has been developed to help participants realize that difference is positive and that we do not all need to be subsumed into one (White) culture. Do not let on to participants that this is the purpose of the exercise until the end of the exercise!

The meal test

Ask each person to imagine the following scenario:

- You are a member of a club or organization. That club expresses its identity and togetherness by means of a weekly formal meal. The meal is held on a specific day and time in the week, every week.
- Every member of the club is invited to the meal and has a major decision to make when they arrive at the entrance of the room where the meal is being held. You can now choose between two meals, and as a member there is no difference in cost, and everyone eats together:
  1. On the one hand, you can choose the 'set meal'. This is the standard accepted meal. It has already been prepared and is already on the menu.
  2. Alternatively, you can eat your favourite meal. This has been prepared for you in exactly the way you want and has been cooked to perfection.
- Which meal do you choose? The one everyone else might be eating or your own special meal? You have absolute choice, and as a full member of the club, you are there at the meal on the same terms as everyone else. Which meal?

Instructions for the facilitators

- The group are never told what the standard meal is, but do tell them that:
  1. At any given time most of the members of the club will be eating the standard meal as many do not have a favourite or could not be bothered to choose it.
  2. The meal is thought to be perfectly acceptable to and adequate for most of the existing members.
- The facilitator should stand in front of each individual as they are asked the question and repeat the following phrase: 'Are you really sure you want to choose that meal?' (whether it is their favourite or the standard). The purpose of doing this is to put doubt into the mind of each individual. Part of the aim of the facilitator is to get them to change their mind.
- When you have asked the question a number of times, go back through the conversations. Who chose what? Who changed their minds? How many stuck with their favourite meal?

- Why did certain individuals change their minds? What was the relationship between the standard and the favourite meal?
- Does everyone need to eat the same meal in order for the club to be united? What happens if everyone decides to eat their favourite meal?

Reflecting on the exercise

The above exercise has been used on numerous occasions in formal educational settings (theological/seminary students training for ordained ministry) or informal ones (lay people in adult education groups in local churches). On those occasions when I have used it a number of salient features have emerged from the resultant reflections.

We choose certain meals because they suit us, we like them, they meet our needs. Those meals say something about our culture and personality. They speak of an emotional response, a sense of identity. We all want to be fed in a manner that meets our needs. For those who chose their favourite meal, it in no way represents a disparaging of the other meal. Simply, it is an expression of one's preference, for that which is authentic and preferable to that individual.

This exercise serves as a metaphorical way of entering into the dynamics of 'race', power and difference, which have always bedevilled Christian communities and the Church as a whole. Often, in order to deal with the fractures of 'race', ethnicity, gender and sexuality (as we shall see them arise in the exercises in the later chapters of this book), Christian theology has sought to spiritualize the central heart of the gospel. This spiritualization has been effected in order to overcome notions of physical or embodied difference, which often asserted a form of White, Euro-American normality in the propagation and interpretation of the gospel.

This can be seen in the way in which the standard meal is surreptitiously (or not so subtly depending upon how the exercise has been enacted) used as the norm by which the various favourite meals are defined. The favourite is invariably challenged and undermined by the facilitator.

In the exercise, food is the metaphor for culture and humanity. Too often, the wider societies in many predominantly White Western countries have neither reflected nor met the cultural and emotional world of Black people. While some have utilized Black cultural practices, such as tapping into their music, popular culture, fashion, art, expression and so on (often for commercial gain), they have not affirmed the peoples themselves.[2]

Some people may have chosen to eat the standard meal. If that was their choice and they genuinely do not mind not giving up their favourite and would really prefer to eat the standard meal, then that is fine. But there are many Black people who would genuinely prefer to eat their favourite meal but cannot bring themselves to admit this in public for fear of being identified as being 'separatist' or accused of not wanting to 'integrate'.

Often, in White majority Christian-influenced societies, the emphasis is upon 'integration' and a 'colour-blind' doctrine as a means of handling contentious issues of difference. In the context of the meal-test exercise this involves Black people being persuaded to eat the standard meal; that is, to be less like themselves and to be the same as that which is characterized as the standard or the norm, namely White people. This move is often demanded of them in order that we may all be one. In effect, for the body of Christ to function as one unified entity it is necessary that the 'meal' become one where differences are sublimated and, rather, a homogeneous 'standard' is effected, where alternative meals (represented difference in terms of 'race' and ethnicity are ignored) are coercively outlawed by pressure from those with power (the seemingly genial host). When I have been the facilitator I have often played the genial host mirroring the often surreptitious way racism operates in the UK[i] – often through an implicit conflation of alleged 'high culture', cultural norms and traditions

[i] It is interesting to note that the bulk of racism and racial discrimination in the UK has often been built on seemingly concealed forms of 'English manners' and spurious politeness as opposed to legal sanctions explicitly forbidding people to exercise their full civic and human rights. It is worth noting that, in post-war British history, there were no laws *preventing* Black and Asian people from buying property in certain areas. Yet the ethic of concealment and manners had the same effect on Black settlement patterns as could be found in such contexts as the USA or South Africa, where explicit statutory provisions existed. In the meal test the participants are never told they cannot eat their favourite; but sufficient pressure is applied to render that choice an incorrect or even a forbidden one. For an interesting look at the backdrop to the seeming veneer of mannered racism in the UK, see David Isiorho, 'Black Theology, Englishness and the Church of England' in Michael N. Jagessar and Anthony G. Reddie (eds), *Postcolonial Black British Theology* (Peterborough: Epworth Press, 2007), pp. 62–72. See also John L. Williams, *Michael X: A Life in Black and White* (London: Century, 2008), pp. 43–77.

('We've always done it like this') and a seemingly polite but nevertheless insistent imposition that one 'becomes more like us' in order to belong.

Marginalized and oppressed people get it every time

Perhaps the most striking point to make is the fact that those who are marginalized or oppressed within many Western societies, whether on grounds of 'race' (the central point of departure in this study), gender, class, sexuality or disability, have immediately caught sight of the underlying truth of the metaphor. The meal test is not about a meal. It has been interesting to witness the number of predominantly White, middle-class, articulate males (particularly clergy) who have been, as we say in Britain, 'a little slow on the uptake', meaning they have not caught on very quickly.

If those who are representative of powerful, privileged and advantaged backgrounds do not 'catch on' very quickly, then why should that be the case?

The answer I believe lies in the experiential subjectivity of those on the margins. It is my contention that those who are marginalized have, through their enforced position and experience, learnt how to operate within a double-consciousness framework. This is one where the repressed and marginalized subject is able to 'read' the values of the dominant world while juxtaposing this often enforced reality alongside their innate subjectivity. Charles Foster and Fred Smith see notions of double consciousness as an essential paradigm and narrative thread in the work of Grant Shockley, one of the pioneers of a liberative approach to Christian education in the African American experience.[3]

The failure of often White middle-class professionals to see what was happening in the exercise has for me, as the facilitator and educator, been an interesting point of analysis. In the first instance, this form of reversal of the normal locus or location of authority within the dynamic of community formation is reflective of some of my previous work in the area of pedagogy in Christian learning contexts.[4] In fact I would assert that one of the most powerful and important 'learning outcomes' of this exercise has been the extent to which those with power who normally predominate in the usual dynamics that govern community formation are often the ones who feel disadvantaged in this seemingly innocent experiential exercise. As I will demonstrate when reflecting on the important transformative truths to be discerned from this exercise, the very reversal of these habitual and seemingly fixed constructed norms of White normality and hegemony (or all-embracing power) are reversed – if only in part. *The first can become last and the last become first.*

Those who are used to having their perspectives construed as at best 'second best', and are often completely demonized and without worth, are usually the ones who see the truths of the exercise with greater clarity, and are usually some time in advance of their more powerful and privileged peers. When the facilitator stands before the participant and asks repeatedly, 'Are you sure you want to choose that favourite meal? Are you really, really sure? The standard meal is ever so sophisticated and I am sure you would like it much better than your perfectly nice, I am sure, favourite meal', most Black folk know that type of discourse like a form of hypnotic mantra.

As a Black British-born citizen, I have grown up with the allegedly 'well-intentioned' rhetoric of integration ringing in my ears, which has sought to convince me that my own cultural heritage and ethnically derived practices were somehow deficient and lacking sophistication. In the politely veneered climate of British racism, this form of effortless cultural superiority is not spelt out in the visceral and polemical terms that have characterized the USA. Rather, within the British context the politeness of the rhetoric has sought to disguise the underlying ethnocentric and patrician arrogance of White institutional power.

The experience of marginalized peoples in the context of the exercise is one that attempts to mirror the dynamics and realities of many societies in the West. Many of us have been on the receiving end of subtle and not so oblique forms of cultural superiority at the hands of White elitism. Black cultural forms, at once exotic or commercially rewarding, are also significantly less aesthetically pleasing or august than the material practices of White power. While some of the normal power imbalances are reversed within the reflective processes of the exercise, it is important that I also report that the experiential dynamics of the participative framework also contain an inbuilt ambivalence in the actions of the various players.

Although marginalized individuals are usually quicker in gaining a sense of the learning outcomes of the exercise, such insights arise at the conclusion of the collaborative engagement. In the construction of the exercise I created an internal dynamic in which the facilitator is expected to pressurize and intimidate the participants when interrogating them over their choice for standard meal or favourite meal. The subtle pressure imposed upon various participants is intended to mirror the didactic function of the media, which in its assertion of White globalized power structures negates the values and counter-claims of other epistemologies or forms of truth and knowledge.[5] When the exercise has been enacted I have noted the extent to which participants' ability to insist upon their choice of the favourite meal when confronted by the facilitator is linked to their social status and educational background.

When older Black people, such as those who belong to the 'Windrush' generation (Black people who travelled from the Caribbean to the UK during the post-Second World War epoch), have been challenged about the legitimacy of their choice of the favourite meal, most have simply acquiesced. White European notions of superiority and models of miseducation of Black people have led to many of these older Black people imbibing the falsehoods of White supremacy at the expense of their own subjectivity.[6]

Josiah Young has described the continued influence and appeal of White images of Jesus as opposed to Black ones or postcolonial images in many rural African American churches.[7] Young's concerns are directed at older African Americans in the southern states of the USA, whose theological disposition seems to have remained untouched despite the signific-ance of both the Civil Rights and the Black Power movements of the 1960s. This preference for seemingly standardized, obliquely White-orientated norms is rejected among many younger Black people, however. When I have played the facilitator in the exercise and chal-lenged younger Black people on their choice of the favourite or the standard meal they have invariably refused to recant, even if their initial choice has been for their favourite (culturally Black) meal. When White powerful people have been challenged they rarely change their minds. The power of White socio-cultural norms is such that there is a firm conviction of their rightness – a self-consciously constructed exercise does not break their equilibrium.[8]

For many professional White middle-class men taking part in this exercise, it is not unlike the substantive elemental features of their everyday existence. For them, this exercise and having to choose what they want or whether they will forgo on their choices is not unlike the common everyday occurrences of life. White men with power often get to choose. Black women, particularly those who are poor, according to Black British Womanist,[ii] Lorraine Dixon, are rarely afforded that luxury.[9]

In a limited sense, this exercise has been important in simply reminding many White people of their inherited advantages just from being White. When maleness, class, sexuality and education are also factored into the equation it should come as no surprise to realize that particular individuals invariably transpose their existential realities into the context of a constructed exercise.

In using this exercise it has been my intention to construct the meal test as an experiential model or a distancing process, to critically engage adult participants in an emotional or psychological (what one might say is a dialectical process) struggle to critically reframe their consciousness or awareness in terms of their engagement with their wider environment and context. The semantic 'game playing' is very much embedded within the framework of the exercise. As the participants begin to immerse themselves in the exercise they come to see that the 'meal' is both real and imaginary. The exercise was about a meal, but also about the wider realities of which we are all a part.

[ii] Womanist theology is a thematic and methodological approach to the task of talking about and reflecting on the meaning of God in light of the experiences, realities and ways of knowing that arise from the particularity of being a Black woman. Womanist theology arises from the term Womanist coined by Alice Walker in her 1984 book, *In Search of Our Mother's Garden: Womanist Prose* (London: Women's Press, 1984). The term refers to the audacity and precocious nature of young Black girls, who might be said to be acting too 'womanish' by their forebears. The audacity and gifted nature of Black women's experiences and sense of hope is further explored in Walker's most famous book, *The Colour Purple* (London: Women's Press, 1983). For other significant Womanist theology texts, see Delores Williams, *Sisters in the Wilderness: The Challenge of Womanist God-Talk* (Maryknoll: Orbis, 1993); Kelly Brown Douglas, *The Black Christ* (New York: Orbis, 1994); Emile Townes, *Womanist Justice, Womanist Hope* (Atlanta: Scholars Press, 1993); Renita J. Weems, *Just a Sister Away: A Womanist Vision of Women's Relationships in the Bible* (Philadelphia: Innisfree Press, 1988); Katie G. Cannon, *Black Womanist Ethics* (Atlanta: Scholars Press, 1988); Stacey M. Floyd-Thomas, *Mining the Motherlode: Methods in Womanist Ethics* (Cleveland: Pilgrim Press, 2006); Stacey M. Floyd-Thomas (ed.), *Deeper Shades of Purple: Womanism in Religion and Society* (New York: New York University Press, 2006); and Emilie M. Townes, *Womanist Ethics and the Cultural Production of Evil* (New York: Palgrave Macmillan, 2006).

Theological reflections

The meal test and the resultant reflections have been performed on numerous occasions since it was first developed in the autumn/fall of 1995. In fact this was the first ever experiential exercise I developed when I began my doctoral studies at the University of Birmingham. These were concerned with developing an interdisciplinary approach to Black theological discourse by means of an African-centred approach to Christian education. In developing this exercise I was concerned with finding an interactive and accessible means of enabling ordinary people (both Black and White) to look critically at the common framework of church and the incipient theology and traditions that underpinned this collective entity called the body of Christ. I witnessed at first hand ways in which 'race' remained a corrosive factor in the practice of the Christian faith among mono-cultural and more pluralistic faith communities, and yet was rarely expressed or even acknowledged.

Growing up in a predominantly White church I remember quite clearly the rhetoric of 'we don't see colour' and yet seeing the ways in which 'colour' so patently informed the very basis of how groups of people engaged with one another.

It should be the case that the meal test (in which the meal is meant to be a metaphor for the Church and for the wider society) allows each person to choose their own individual meal and to enjoy it while sitting alongside their neighbour who is presently enjoying their own particular favourite meal. The kingdom of God is a diverse one. God who has inspired all people to be themselves has created this diversity.[10] Think how boring it would be if at that meal everyone chose the same standard meal. There would be no variety or difference. Unity does not mean that we all have to be the same. If that were what God had intended then we would have all been created exactly alike. The ideal at that meal (and for the Church also) is everyone sitting down at that gathering eating their own favourite meal, with each person having the opportunity to sample bits from the favourite meals of other people sitting around them. That is, people learning from each other – our differences not separating us, but in actual fact bringing us all together. For me, this metaphor represents the central ideal that is the kingdom of God.

The body of Christ is about recognizing difference. The body should be concerned with providing opportunities for all marginalized and oppressed peoples to have their choices, preferences and identities recognized, and for the existing power structures to be overturned in order that those elements can be realized.

In taking the meal as a metaphor for the Church, Black Christians must seek to work in partnership with other agencies of faith and none, in order to proclaim the radical message of the kingdom of God that is not reducible to personal piety and individual notions of being saved. Beckford has identified the limited basis of this form of theological construction in an influential publication.[11]

When Henry McNeal Turner, one of the early leaders of the Black-identified African Methodist Episcopal Church[iii] stated in 1895 that 'God is a negro' he did so not as a form of 'reverse racism' against White people but rather as a proclamation of the radical, iconoclastic nature of Christianity, which should stand against all the 'accepted logic' of vested interests and narrow sectarian notions of election.[12] Turner was writing at a time when the majority of White Christians saw no contradiction between being Christian and advocating notions of White superiority. I would contest that there are very few examples of White Christians at the time Turner was writing (even those who fought against the slave trade) who believed in Black equality with Whites!

Alongside Turner, one can point to other scholars who have sought to appropriate faith from within a Black cultural and his-

[iii] Due to the endemic racism of Euro-Americans in the seventeenth and eighteenth centuries, many Black Christians left the established White-dominated and -run denominations in order to found their own Churches. This movement gave rise to the historic Black Church in the USA. The Churches that fall into this designation and tradition are, the African Methodist Episcopal Church (AME), the African Methodist Episcopal Zion Church (AMEZ), the Christian Methodist Church (CME), the National Baptist Convention Incorporated, the National Baptist Convention of America, the Progressive Baptist Convention and the Church of God in Christ. For further information, see E. Eric Lincoln and Lawrence H. Mamiya, *The Black Church in the African American Tradition* (Durham, North Carolina: Due University Press, 1991). See also Anne H. Pinn and Anthony B. Pinn, *Black Church History* (Minneapolis: Fortress Press, 2002). See also Delroy A. Reid-Salmon for a Caribbean-influenced notion of a Diasporan Church in America, which is different from the named Churches above, both in its genealogy and in the ethnic composition of its theological and cultural identity – Reid-Salmon, *Home Away From Home: The Caribbean Diasporan Church in the Black Atlantic Experience* (London: Equinox, 2008).

torical framework in order to bolster the sense of connectedness for Black people and their God-given Blackness.[13] Edward Blyden used Christian teachings and a nascent Black theology as his means of responding to the need for Black affirmations of the self. As an African-centred scholar of the late nineteenth century, Blyden put the case for an awareness and appreciation of the African roots of Black culture and identity as a means of asserting the selfhood of people of African descent. Blyden amplified this thesis by arguing that Africa's service to the world and to Christendom in particular laid siege to any fallacious doctrine enshrining the inferiority of Black people.[14] Blyden makes this point most eloquently when he writes:

> To any one who has travelled in Africa, especially in the portion north of the equator, extending from the West Coast to Abyssinia, Nubia and Egypt, and embracing what is known as the Nigritian and Soudanic countries, there cannot be the slightest doubt as to the country and people to whom the terms Ethiopia and Ethiopian, as used in the Bible and the classical writers, were applied . . . Africans were not unknown, therefore, to the writers of the Bible. Their peculiarities of complexion and hair were as well known to the ancient Greeks and Hebrews, as they are to the American people today. And when they spoke of the Ethiopians, they meant the ancestors of the black-skinned and woolly-haired people who, for two hundred and fifty years, have been known as labourers on the plantations of the South.[15]

Challenging cultural racism

What the exercise also demonstrates is the subtle nature of cultural racism. In using this term, what I mean to suggest is that the sense of White Euro-American superiority over Black Africans takes its cue from the notion that the cultural practices and traditions of the former are superior to those of the latter.[16] This form of 'new racism' is one that largely moves beyond the genetic-based rhetoric of White superiority that characterized 'old racism' to a cultural and aesthetic model for a top-down patrician or class-based notion of Euro-American hegemony or power.

In my most recent work I have argued that one of the most pressing challenges that still faces us in our contemporary postmodern epoch is the need to engage with the realities of racial injustice as it affects the Church and those beyond its good offices.[17] I believe it is still the case that Black people know far more about White people than the reverse. My intention is not to traduce or attack White people in any simplified and generic sense, but Black experience that gives rise to Black Christianity is one that must challenge White people to face up to the unearned privileges accrued from Whiteness. Robert Beckford states that:

> Because whiteness and white people are not 'racialised' in the same way as other groups, whiteness is able to function as an ethnically neutral category that can go unexplored and unchallenged as the standard for expectation and evaluation . . . For many black people in Britain today, to be accepted as 'normal' in white dominated circles of power and influence requires a sacrifice of aspects of black identity and culture.[18]

In response to the realities thus described by Beckford, Black theology must resist the temptation to retreat into colour-blind notions of faith and theology. Black Christianity and Black theology came into being by both recognizing and affirming colour and difference,[19] but opposing the strictures of fixed identity and 'race'[20] as constructed from within the ranks of Euro-American Enlightenment thought.[21] The conservative elements in Black Churches in Britain, particularly those from within the Pentecostal tradition, have always found it a little unsettling to explicitly engage with the theological and sociological substance of Blackness. Robert Beckford's work in Britain has proved to be the most notable exception.[22] Many have opted for a colour-blind approach in their engagement with the Christian faith. In a previous text, I have argued against notions of colour-blind theology as a means of Black Christians and Black Churches expressing their Christian faith and resulting praxis or reflective action.[23]

Affirming difference – affirming Blackness

The colour-blind approach of which I speak is one that does not see colour in its hermeneutical or interpretive engagement with the Christian faith. This particular approach works from the basis that God is Spirit and that 'in Christ' there is no discernible physical difference in terms of identity and materiality (Galatians 3.28).

As African American theologians Pinn and Hopkins[24] have demonstrated, and more latterly, Womanist theologian Kelly Brown Douglas,[25] Black Christianity, drawing on the dualistic modes of thinking developed by Greek antiquity and largely propagated through Pauline theology, has encouraged many Black people to downplay or even despise the materiality of their Black bodies. Basically, Christianity has taught many Black people to be suspicious of our Blackness. When I have asked some Black participants in the meal-test exercise to state which meal they would choose to eat, a number have stated that they want to eat the standard meal. When I have probed for the reasons for doing so (after they have already told me how much they love their favourite meal and would love to eat it), some have remarked, 'We don't want to make a fuss' or, 'I want to be like all the others' – the ones eating the standard meal.

What is interesting to note in these responses is the underlying perception and notion that it is Blackness and being Black itself that is the problem. Now, at one level I can understand the temptation to withdraw into the theology that underpins colour-blind practices within the Church. If seeing Black is to see negativity, second-class status, bestiality, limited humanity and lesser intelligence, then quite naturally I would rather people not see my colour at all. If Black can only be perceived in negative terms then there is some logic in the persuasiveness of colour-blind doctrines, and as such these thought-forms can appear to have their worth.

The problem with such thinking, however, is that it still preserves the dichotomy between White being neutral and normative and Black being 'the other' or something to be overlooked or even transcended. Black theology wants to argue for the particularity of Blackness; meaning that it is in our very Blackness that God is not only revealed, but also understood within the realms of our Blackness and the experiences that emerge from being Black. I want people to see my Blackness. God created me as a Black man and I do not believe for one second that God made a mistake in doing so. So when you see me, please see me as a Black male; but ascribe to my Blackness the positive elements that have traditionally been reserved for Whiteness and White people.

Colour-blind approaches when they are practised by Black people actually run against the weight of historical evidence as to the development of Black Christianity, which in turn has helped to give rise to Black theology. This more conservative colour-blind doctrine that is the underlying theology of some Black Christians is at variance with the radical intent of Black theology.

The radical appropriation of Blackness lies at the heart of the Black theology enterprise. James Cone, who remains the most visible and consistent spokesperson for the radical intent of Black theology from within a Christian framework, states that: 'In a society that defines blackness as evil and whiteness as good, the theological significance of Jesus is found in the possibility of human liberation through blackness. Jesus is the black Christ.'[26] Black Christians need to learn to affirm their favourite meals in the meal test. They need to reclaim a radical Black Christology first espoused with great eloquence by James Cone.[27] Cone writes of Jesus:

> It seems clear that the overwhelming weight of biblical teaching, especially the prophetic tradition in which Jesus stood unambiguously, is upon God's unqualified identification with the poor precisely because they are poor. The kingdom of God is for the helpless, because they have no security in this world. We see this emphasis in the repeated condemnation of the rich, notably the Sermon on the Mount . . . Jesus' teaching about the kingdom is the most radical, revolutionary aspect of his message.[28]

The very intentionality of Jesus' praxis acts as a counterbalance to the non-contextual and often abstracted theologies of predominantly prosperity-led practitioners of Black Christianity as seen in the likes of Creflo Dollar[29] in the USA and Matthew Ashimolowo in the UK.[30] Jesus engages with the context in which he is located, in a real and embodied way, and does not retreat into spiritual banalities as a means of avoiding being labelled 'political'.[31]

The politics of difference are always at play in any historical context and they demand an honest appraisal from the Christian faith. It can be argued that the radical nature of Jesus' ministry was the clear intentional approach of his teaching to questions of difference and acceptability, particularly in terms of who is deemed 'one of us' (and therefore all right) and who 'one of them' (and in oppositional terms to be treated with suspicion or something stronger).

One can see aspects of this in terms of how 'we' have all been manipulated into thinking of those who are different in very subtle ways that still emphasize their unacceptability. Black theology challenges head-on any attempt to make Blackness acceptable by stealth – that is, only some of us can be deemed acceptable within the club and the accompanying meal, but only if we show ourselves to be worthy of that honour by being 'extraordinarily good' (I have named this the Sidney Poitier syndrome)[iv] or somehow possessed of the magic ability to transcend our Blackness.

One can see aspects of this 'stealth' process as I have described it by looking at a seemingly innocuous passage from the synoptic gospels.

A Black-theology reading of Luke 10.29–37

After discussing the meal test and reflecting on affirming difference it may be helpful to follow with a Bible study. This Black-theology rereading of Luke 10.29–37 begins with a personal confession (they are meant to be good for the soul, so here goes!). While an undergraduate student at university I was a member of a Christian street-theatre group; indeed, it was the experience of acting out the gospel through drama that gave rise to my later interest in drama as a means of undertaking Black theology.[32] Our group once performed a radically alternative version of this famous parable of the Good Samaritan. The parable had already been adapted by the Christian dramatists Paul Burbridge and Murray Watts of the Riding Lights Theatre Company.[33] In their rewritten version the Samaritan becomes a punk rocker.

In our restyled version, the punk rocker becomes a Rastafarian, with yours truly wearing an unfeasibly large stuffed, multicoloured leg warmer on my head in my truly criminally embarrassing role as the 'good dread'. Oh, how I have wished I could go back and tell my stupid 20-year-old self the folly of such a politically incorrect travesty of cultural stereotyping.

[iv] The Sidney Poitier syndrome, as I have termed it, takes its cue from his landmark 1967 film, *Guess Who's Coming to Dinner*. Poitier plays a highly respected African American medical doctor of impeccable credentials who is engaged to be married to a young White woman. The drama of the film emerges when the latter brings her Black fiancé home to meet her liberal White parents. While the film was a landmark production when it came out in 1967, one is still left with the clear sense that Poitier's character had to be saint-like simply to get to make it with a relatively unspectacular White woman (who lacks his great accomplishments).

The main theological problem with our retelling and with that of the source material from the book, *Time to Act*,[34] is the very popularized title of the parable as we have come to know it. A casual survey of over ten different versions of the Bible in the chapel at the Queen's Foundation alerted me to the fact that all of them titled this parable 'The Good Samaritan'. On the face of it, this parable seems to offer a relatively straightforward moral for all who would seek to describe themselves as Christians. The parable challenges us to exercise pastoral care and concern for all people irrespective of whatever cultural differences or religious niceties or customs that might impede such actions. The priest and the Levite who walk on the other side and who do not attend to the beaten man left half dead on the road seem more concerned with religious and cultural niceties connected with the need not to render themselves unclean. The need to preserve the prevailing religious and cultural norms is more important than acting in an inclusive and supportive manner in attending to a man gravely in need of assistance and support.

And yet, in naming the 'hero' in this passage as 'good', irrespective of whether he is a Samaritan, a punk rocker or a Rastafarian, the subtle framework of this title is one that by a matter of stealth confirms the unacceptability and lesser status of the person who is different rather than confounding it. Let me explain this remark. In the parable, it is undoubtedly the case that the Samaritan, or the punk rocker or the Rastafarian, is the 'good guy'. Yet in labelling them 'good' do we not imply that *most* Samaritans, punk rockers or Rastafarians are not good?

Cain Hope Felder, in his commentary on Luke's Gospel, writing on this passage states:

> The Samaritan of Extraordinary Mercy – One should avoid calling this passage 'the Good Samaritan' as if most of them were not good. African Americans have known the subtle humiliation of being dubbed 'a good Negro'. This parable epitomizes the enormous value of those irrespective of their station in life being able to 'love their enemies' due to a deep spirituality that transcends religiosity and legalisms. The Samaritan that Jesus sets forth in this parable is a man of unusual spirituality who has the true understanding of God's mercy to others. Although Jesus' disciples had earlier wanted to have the Samaritans destroyed, Jesus shows them through this Samaritan 'a still more excellent way'. In fact, Jesus makes the Samaritan a teacher of the disciples![35]

Speaking as a Black male I am very much aware of the way in which society labels Black people in general, and Black men in particular, as often amoral degenerates. We are trouble-makers and undesirables; but some of us, of course, can be acceptable. If we have the right accent, can mimic the cultural mores of polite White middle-class society, then we too can be invited to the meal and thereby pass the meal test. The Good Samaritan becomes a culturally acceptable version of Blackness not unlike the popularized images of the Huxtables as portrayed in *The Cosby Show* or the Banks in their portrayal in *The Fresh Prince of Bel-Air.*

Both these highly successful shows (running from 1984–92 and 1990–6 respectively on NBC television) presented an aspiring image of Black social mobility and acceptability. In both shows one witnesses idealized and, dare one say, acceptable notions of Blackness; images that can be considered sufficiently 'good' (like the Samaritan, the punk rocker or the Rastafarian) to be invited to the 'meal' of White corporate America. In my own life I have witnessed how my own acceptability to be welcomed in the meal, alongside the polite, the acceptable, the educated, the socially desirable and the respectable middle-class, has been in direct proportion to my social mobility by way of higher education and further study. My own acceptability within the formal meal, as one who is able to eat the standard meal as well as my favourite, is testament to the progress I have made in terms of social and occupational mobility.[36] But what if my working-class Yorkshire accent had not taken on the trappings of middle-class modulation and university-educated sophistry? Would I still be so willingly embraced within the meal? Would the standard meal still be forced upon me as a mode of making me suitably civilized so that I can become an authentic part of the meal and the formal membership of the club that accompanies it? Writing as a Methodist, I am reminded of the charge levelled by Theodore Jennings, who argues that Methodism of the contemporary era struggles to emulate the inclusive and transformative practice of its founder, whose commitment to the transformation of the poor saw him transcend most of the social and cultural boundaries of respectability and conformity that were replete within the comfortable (largely Anglican) landed gentry of eighteenth-century England.[37]

For Black Christians sitting in the meal, we must not only be sufficiently brave to argue for the eating of the types of foods that give us life and sustain us, we must also resist the temptation to be the 'good Black person' who will opt to eat the standard meal simply to become acceptable to others. A radical nature of difference strikes us immediately when reading Luke 10. It reminds us of the unacceptability of the Samaritan to orthodox Jewish people, and yet he is the one who Jesus uses to teach the lesson of the 'Jesus way' to others. The Samaritan does not suddenly become more Jewish because he did the right thing. On the contrary, he remains the other, and yet he is united with the person he helped by means of his act of justice and mercy – that is, doing the right thing as opposed to necessarily believing the right thing. (In Liberation theologies this dichotomy between doing the right thing and believing the right thing is termed orthopraxis versus orthodoxy.) Our acceptability should be judged on the grounds of how we engage with others and whether we are in solidarity with those who are 'the least of these', and not on how well we used our metaphorical knives and forks and whether we decide to eat the standard meal, in order to show that we are good Samaritans, punk rockers or Rastafarians.

The same meal, different food

In conclusion, then, if we take the meal test as a metaphor for the Church, then the question becomes: How and in what ways is the practice of racial justice in evidence within the intentional life of this faith-based community? Is the meal expressed in terms of some being coerced into self-negation as a means of being 'one' in the community? Does the community that enjoys the meal operate on the tacit 'new racism' of assuming that the standard meal is superior, of greater quality and more in keeping with the refined and 'civilized' nature of the club?

If we translate this metaphor into one that now speaks of the Church, is it the case that for Black people to co-exist with White people within the body of Christ, we have to reject our favourite meals as opposed to celebrating and rejoicing in them? Can we move to the point where as Black people we are not seen as problems but rather as opportunities for celebrating God's uniqueness as it is expressed and experienced in and through cultural difference?

The historic faith of Black people in the African Diaspora emerged from dispiriting and dehumanizing contexts in the so-called New

World, but has reached the point where we now occupy significant cultural and social spaces within the globalized economy of many Western Churches. In my own ecclesial context, the British Methodist Church, all the fastest-growing churches are Black majority ones. The growth and development from the submerged underground railway and concealed gatherings to the mega-church phenomenon of postmodernity is testament to the tenacity and perseverance of Black people across the world.

Yet the challenge that now confronts Black Christians is the need to constantly re-engage with the existential realities of the bulk of all Black peoples across the world whose life-experiences and realities remain stunted and blighted by the twin terrors of racism and economic poverty. It remains one of calling White hegemony to task and offering a radical version of Christian faith that will inspire and transform the thinking and action of all people, especially that of Black young people in postcolonial Britain.

Now is not the time for attempting to cling on to the coat-tails of the White establishment or fall for the blandishments of those who espouse the rhetoric of a White Christian supremacist new world order. As one can witness from the meal test, what unites us is the fact that all are committed to sharing a meal together as one set of people rather than the notion that all of us have to eat the same meal.

Just as many radical and socially committed White Christians are campaigning for an alternative to this so-called new world order,[38] Black Christians must join forces with these radical voices while remaining vigilant to challenge the often unspoken and unacknowledged White privilege of those who profess to be in solidarity with the Black voiceless poor of the world.[39]

The meal test is a metaphor for the Church and how we attempt to work out our sense of collective identity – in terms of sameness and difference within the body of Christ. From my varied performances of this exercise with participants of differing ethnicities, it has become clear to me that it is our shared reflections on this experiential activity that have alerted us to the often tacit nature of power that exists within the collective and corporate nature of the meal/Church. Oftentimes, an unspoken and tacit Whiteness, represented by the standard meal, becomes the normative template that is used to judge and categorize all others. On only one occasion have I heard a participant say, 'And tell me, who decides that the standard meal should be the standard?' Who indeed? And who decided that essentially White Eurocentric thought-forms should become the standard basis on which we judge Christian orthodoxy?[40]

The best response I have received from the many occasions I have used this exercise came from an elderly Caribbean man who said, 'I would hope that I could eat my favourite meal in the club and that others would choose their favourite meals also. Then I could enjoy the meal I love to eat, but could then take bits off other people's plates and also enjoy what they are eating as well!'

I can think of no better way of describing the kingdom of God in metaphorical terms!

2

Proverbial wisdom: the ongoing quest for racial justice

The task of challenging racism and working for racial justice is one that requires Black people to draw upon their historic resources of wisdom and spiritual reflection as the means of 'deciphering the truth of the world'. This chapter is concerned with empowering Black people in the constant necessity to continue resisting racism in all forms and complex guises.[1] While Chapter 3 is aimed at challenging and assisting predominantly White people to engage with the pernicious invisibility that is Whiteness,[2] this chapter is directed at predominantly Black people and the need for them to affirm their Blackness and the cultures and spiritual resources that have emerged from ongoing experiences of struggle.

I return here, in part, to some of my earlier work where I argued that a central task for a practical model of Black theology was to assist Black youth in interpreting the veracity of the world that faced them.[3] That is, to assist Black young people to discover what is the truthful action of Jesus Christ that can set them free in a racially troubled and divided world.[4]

This chapter proceeds on the basis that true wisdom is a gift from God and is a product of experience[5] – in our ongoing lives with God, we come to experience and know truth in the context of our relationship with God and with significant others. The following is taken from one of my books, *Dramatizing Theologies*,[6] where I state:

> It has often been asserted that many Black people have prioritised the experience of God over and above notions of conceptual or cerebral knowledge about God.[7] In this respect, given that the process of gaining direct access to the transformative experience of God is open to all people, this form of knowledge production and epistemology[i] can be seen as a democratisation of ultimate truth – the truth of God.[8]

[i] This word simply means 'how we know what we know to be true' – i.e. how do we come to know what is truth?

The quotation sums up one of the most important subtexts (underlying theories that guide that which sits on the surface of our thinking) of this chapter, namely, that Black people, through our encounter with oppressive power throughout history, have learnt to reread and interpret the world by means of our accessing the presence and power of God in the world. That power is the Spirit of God.

The accessing of the presence and the power of God in the lives of Black people often takes expression in the ability to sense what is truthful about the people one encounters in the daily routine of life. I am reminded of a conversation with my maternal grandmother, a Jamaican woman who was born and died in a region named East Portland. She was not a learned woman by the standards of the present day and yet she had a remarkable gift of being able to 'suss out' the motives and truths of others.

On the occasions she met people she did not trust (and therefore did not care for), she would say out of earshot of that person, 'Mi spirit noh tek to dem'. The phrase in English (it is spoken in Jamaican) means, 'My spirit does not find favour with that person'. In using this phrase, my grandmother, like many before her, was invoking a deep-seated wisdom of Black (in this case Caribbean) people who have been able to fuse orthodox Christian faith with African-derived religions in a manner that holds together the present and past.[9] This 'present' and the 'past' represent the Christian raditions that emerged in many diasporan African peoples (those taken in captivity and removed from Africa to the Caribbean by slavery) and the historic African traditions that accompanied them across the Atlantic.[10]

In using this spiritualized sense of wisdom that comes from Africa, but which has been moulded and transformed by 400 years of suffering and struggle in the Caribbean, my grandmother (and many others beside) were drawing upon a rich heritage as a means of learning to decipher the perils that accompanied Black Caribbean people in the world of plantation slavery and colonialism. The Black Christian faith of my grandmother, like that of many of her peers, was a complex amalgam of Western evangelical imperial mission theology and largely West African religious traditions. The Black Christianity that emerged in the Caribbean was a response to the reality of oppression.[11] One of the main consequences arising from the Diasporan African experience of slavery, colonialism and reconstruction (in the USA) was the sense that many Black people learnt very quickly that the world was not a place to be trusted. The world of White people was one in which Black communities lived in terms of fear, trepidation and the constant threat of annihilation.[12] Consequently, many Black communities became cautiously conservative in their dealings with White power and used a form of spiritually derived discernment as a means of working out how one engaged with the oppressive and retributive power of English colonialism and empire.

The nature of the threat to Black life was such that no concessions were made in terms of socializing and nurturing children into both the contextual struggles of simply trying to stay alive in a hostile environment while also inculcating in them the necessary survival skills borne out through Christian faith as a means of overcoming these very real environmental threats.

When Caribbean migrants came to Britain in the post-Windrush era (approximately 1948–65),[13] they brought with them this legacy of spiritual wisdom from Africa and the Caribbean. Upon arrival in the UK, these people encountered a great deal of racism.[14] What enabled many of them to cope with their experiences of rejection was a direct sense of God being with them. This 'God with them' is in the form of the Spirit that offers alternative ways of interpreting one's experience and dealing with the reality of rejection and hurt.

An exercise in proverbial wisdom

I have used the following exercise, first developed several years ago but adapted and modified over time,[15] as a means of enabling Black Caribbean participants to reflect upon the nature of how wisdom and knowledge has often operated within African Caribbean religious cultures and history. The sayings were all given to me by older Black, Caribbean Christian women in Birmingham (largely Methodists, Anglicans, Baptists and some Pentecostals) when I was doing my PhD in the late 1990s. The aim of this part of the research was to show how Black proverbial wisdom (wisdom imparted through the medium of wise sayings) can be a resource for the Christian formation and nurture of young Black children. The initial aim of the exercise was to ask Black young people what the meaning of these wise sayings is.

In the exercise I split participants into groups and ask them to interpret the meaning of some of the following 'wise sayings' or 'proverbs' from the Caribbean:

1 ***If yu wan' good, den yu nose mus' run.*** (If you want to prosper, or move forward, then you will have to make some form of sacrifice or have to work for what you want.)
2 ***If yu 'ave ears fi 'ear, but cyaan 'ear, den yu mus' feel.*** (If you have been given an opportunity to learn something, or have been given a warning, but refuse to listen or heed the advice, then you will have to feel the consequences, and then will learn the hard way.)
3 ***Yu mus' learn fi dance at home before yu dance abroad.*** (You must first learn how to behave or act at home in front of your family, where your actions will not be held against you. It is better to learn in this environment than to embarrass yourself in the outside world.)
4 ***Wantey wantey nuh getty getty, but getty getty nuh wantey wantey.*** (Very often, when we really want something, we don't always get it. When we finally get that same something, then we no longer want it.)
5 ***If wishes were horses, den beggars wud ride.*** (If wishing for something were all that was required for dreams to come true, then everyone would get what they wanted.)
6 ***De higher de monkey climb is de more 'im get exposed.*** (You may think that you are fooling people with your thoughts, attitude or behaviour, but the higher up the ladder you climb and the more important you become, the more people will see you for what you are.)
7 ***Yu mus' tek sleep mark death.*** (When a particular event or a set of circumstances arises, you should use that as an indication or a pointer for possible worst things that may follow.)
8 ***Tell de trut' an sleep a door!*** (If you tell the truth, you must expect to be thrown out, and made unwelcome.)

In order to encourage discussion and conversation you may wish to challenge participants to reflect critically on their own experiences:

1 Do their own experiences agree with these sayings?
2 Can they think of times when it would have been a good idea to apply this wisdom to their own lives?

3 Do these sayings help them to better understand people's feelings and behaviour?
4 Do they think these sayings are 'true'?
5 How and in what ways is this truth connected to other truths and, ultimately, to God?

Reflecting on the exercise

When I asked the older women who gave me these sayings (most of whom were grandparents who attended inner-city churches in Birmingham) how they learnt these proverbs, they told me that they did so aurally; that is, through hearing them said. The proverbs came alive in the midst of inter-generational, familial contexts where the elders of the community offered the product of their learnt and inherited wisdom for their younger counterparts through the facility of proverbial wisdom.

When I asked in what circumstances the sayings were spoken, one woman said, 'People used these sayings back home in the Caribbean when an older person (usually a mother figure) wanted you to learn something about life from an incident or event that had just taken place.'

This exercise invites participants to reflect not only on what they know but also how they have come to know it. The participants, through conversation and interaction, have to come to an understanding on what they have come to know as truth. But who decides what is true? How do we decide what the meaning contained within the various sayings is? I have sometimes been struck by the extent to which there are interesting regional variations in the different sayings. African Caribbean people whose families come from the different islands have discovered different versions of some of these sayings (that are predominantly Jamaican in origin from my initial research).

So in the context of our conversing, how do we decide whose version is best understood as an authentic rendering of that particular proverb, and does it matter? With whom will we, as individuals and communities, converse in the process of seeking to discern the truth of any wise saying and what that tells us about the world or the society of which we are a part?

The latter point is of significance because many of us choose to inhabit and reside within particular spaces and places with people who are like us and whom we like. What would happen if participants were forced to share their wise sayings and their interpretations of the proverbial truths contained within them with an imagined 'other'?

When using this experiential exercise I have challenged the Black participants to reflect critically on their own experiences. The exercise calls for a profound sense of judgement for the people taking part, for the sense of discernment needed to discover the truth of any situation is one that also calls for interpretive skills of and for understanding the wider world of which they (and others) are a part.

What is the best way of operating for Black people in Britain? It is worth noting that within the British context, racism and White hegemony have not led to complete separation. Rather difference and (in some cases) downright enmity has been contained by the use of parallel realities.[ii] In effect, Black people and White people have separated into tribal territories, in which demographics and geography account for separation, but both remain housed within the one ecclesial body.

Despite the challenges of history and the nuances of differing contexts, the goal of existing and remaining within the same paradigm remains an important challenge for all Christian communities. This exercise highlights the very real challenges that are in evidence when one attempts to exist within a shared context, where all, if only notionally, are engaged in a shared and similar task, but may have radically different ways of recognizing wisdom and interpreting truth.

[ii] Black Methodists, Anglicans and those in the Baptist and Reformed traditions in the UK have not left to form separate Churches, but have attempted to create their own self-identified spaces within the corporate whole. A similar strategy has been used by Black members of White-dominated Churches in Southern Africa. In the British context, see Heather Walton, *A Tree God Planted: Black People in British Methodism* (London: Ethnic Minorities in Methodism Working Group, the Methodist Church, 1984) and John Wilkinson, *Church in Black and White: The Black Christian Tradition in 'Mainstream' Churches in England* (Edinburgh: Saint Andrew Press, 1993). In terms of the latter, see Jean Knighton-Fitt, *Beyond Fear* (Cape Town: Pretext Publishers, 2003).

The function of proverbial wisdom

It is my belief that one can see aspects of proverbial wisdom at work in the Hebrew sacred texts.[16] One may argue that the knowledge-based systems of the ancient near east have more in common with African-derived forms of knowledge than with what emerges from Europe or European-related sources.[17] These wise sayings operate like the proverbs in the Old Testament. They work through relationship, repetition and remembering.[18]

1 **Relationship** – there is always a relationship between the person giving the wise saying and the hearer who receives it. Proverbial wisdom cannot work if there is no relationship between the two. When the wise saying is said, the hearer has to try to work out (a) What is the meaning of the saying? and (b) What is the point of it? Points (a) and (b) are rarely explained, in explicit terms! By this I mean that the person who gives the saying does not usually explain what they have said. Rather, the statement is simply made. The importance of the learning for the hearer is to try to sort out for themselves what the saying means and why it has been said.[19] This is a major part of the cognitive or intellectual learning function of proverbial wisdom – part of the challenge for the recipient of the proverb is to use his or her intellectual abilities to decipher the meaning of the wise saying.[20]
2 **Repetition** aids the hearer in learning about (a) and (b). The hearer comes to understand the meaning and the point of the saying through repeated exposure to it. When it is used well, it is done in context, in response to a particular event or incident from which the speaker wishes the hearer or recipient to learn. When the saying is used over a period of time and is seen to be linked to certain events or incidents, then the hearer comes to an understanding of the meaning and the basis of the wisdom of the proverb.
3 **Remembering** is the final product that enables the proverbial wisdom to take root. When 1 and 2 have been practised on a continual basis, the hearer will begin to link the wisdom from the wise saying with particular lessons about or on life to be learnt and applied in future. *Proverbs are concentrated, applied wisdom for living.* That is, proverbs operate on the basis of an economy of words. Look at how many words are required to explain the proverb compared to the relative lack of words in the proverb itself.

> The proverbs are also applied wisdom – the contexts in which they are used are nearly always related to real-life issues, specific events or situations of concern.

This form of wisdom emerges from experience – it is the daily encounter with the world that gives rise to communities creating wise sayings as a kind of shorthand product of learning that is intended to instruct and guide the hearer. The hearer is *nearly always* younger than the one sharing the proverb.

The theological basis for this form of knowledge emerges from the Old Testament. In Hebrew religious culture, wisdom is often personified as a woman, and Jewish scholars often term this wisdom Sophia.[21] It is interesting to note that in the Bible (see Proverbs 8.1–12, for example) and in African and Caribbean cultures, 'wisdom' as the speaker and teacher of truth is nearly always a woman! It is the wise woman who imparts wisdom to her younger charges and they will learn if (a) they trust and have a relationship with her and (b) they are willing to listen to her wise sayings.

In the context of Old Testament theology, wisdom is relational. That is, it is different from the way many cultures in the West have come to understand knowledge by means of Greek philosophy. In terms of the latter, knowledge (how we come to know what is true – epistemology) is often seen as abstract; it has no form. This form of knowledge is also individualistic, that is, very clever people will sit in libraries or, sometimes, literally towers (probably not made of ivory, however), and will think deep thoughts, trying to wrestle with deep ideas and concepts that they later (if they choose to do so) share with others.

You will notice that I have differentiated between knowledge (knowing things) and wisdom (the process of being wise). In Old Testament theology, wisdom is not the same as knowledge. *Wisdom always contains knowledge, but not all knowledge is necessarily wisdom.* My maternal grandmother, who never left the eastern parishes of Portland and St Thomas in Jamaica and was one of the wisest people I ever met, would talk about certain people being 'educated fools'. By this, she meant that some people (usually wealthy White overseers on the Banana grove that existed close to where she lived) may have been to school, had 'plenty knowledge, but dem nuh know one diam ting' ('They may have plenty of knowledge but they don't know one thing!') They may have been book-smart, but they were dunces when it came to the applied wisdom of how to live and how to treat others.

I want to argue that what has enabled Black people to survive and in some cases (not as many as one would like) to thrive has been our connection with the wisdom of God through the power of the Spirit. This Spirit is not abstract or without form, for 'she' is often manifested in the wisdom of our 'mother figures'.[22] Our mother figures are the ones who often embody wisdom and have been the custodians of the collective wisdom of a set of people as that people attempt to make sense of the world as they experience it.

So what does this mean for predominantly Black people of faith as we seek to make an impact on wider society? It means that we have to acknowledge that a major part of our role is to be the repository of wisdom, which emerges from the collective experience of being human. This wisdom should be deployed by Black people as a means of continuing to call the Church to account. I am not suggesting that White English cultures do not have their share of proverbial wisdom, because they do. Think of such wise sayings as, 'A stitch in time saves nine' or, 'A bird in the hand is worth two in the bush.' But these sayings were made by the poor and the marginalized of their day. These people never ran the Church of England and they don't do so now. The history of different peoples and their accompanying culture across the world shows that richer and more powerful peoples are not only more likely to lose the art of working with proverbial wisdom, but often come to despise it as well, claiming that it lacks sophistication and is superstitious and old-fashioned.[23]

The truth of the last statement can be discerned in the ways in which many of the major Churches in Britain operate in terms of assessing truth and knowledge in their formal operations, particularly in terms of governance and the exercising of power. In the days when I was a regular attendee of the annual Methodist Conference,[iii]

[iii] The annual Methodist Conference is the collective seat of oversight and authority within the British Methodist Church. The Conference, which dates back to the days of John Wesley, is a representative body of people in and through whom authority and accompanying governance of the Church is vested. For further information on the annual Methodist Conference, see Angela Shier-Jones, 'Conferring as Theological Method' in Clive Marsh et al. (eds), *Unmasking Methodist Theology* (London: Continuum, 2004), pp. 82–92.

I was always struck by the acreage of paper that was generated as this week-long ecclesial event concentrated its collective mind on issues of governance within the life of the Church. My argument is not that this was and is in any sense wrong, simply that when Jesus (in whose name Methodism, like all Churches that claim the title of Christian Church, are constituted) sought to share the truths he had received, he told parables – wise stories.[24] He didn't write long reports! Talking of Jesus, Charles Melchert argues that Jesus' parables can be understood as being part of the proverbial wisdom tradition of Judaism;[25] which finds echoes in that found in the more contemporary proverbs many of these older African Caribbean women shared with me many years ago.

In my years sitting through the many debates that characterize the Methodist Conference, I rarely witnessed the use of proverbial wisdom as a means of generating knowledge during an ecclesial conversation. Rather, the learned and the wise often preferred clever and seemingly intellectual forms of argument over making recourse to wise sayings and narratives that contained some form of subversive truth. One might well argue that as Churches develop and 'progress', such as the Methodist Church, there has emerged a kind of intellectual snobbery that has grown to distrust the subversive and intangible qualities of proverbial wisdom. Proverbial wisdom is rarely written down. It is not systematized or structured or written in committees by wise people (usually White Oxbridge men) or scheduled on very long agendas in endless reports. Its very nature seems to militate against its being used in these formal settings, and yet it remains a potent force in many poor, Black Caribbean working-class contexts. I can still point to certain church communities who will not make a formal decision on the future of the church until 'Sister Mary' or 'Sister Rose', the wise old matriarch at the back of the church, has 'testified' – has shared her proverbial wisdom, which becomes the basis of guiding the church in its future, forward trajectory. I can't see that in evidence within corporate Methodism, for example.

Making proverbial wisdom work for us today

In order for proverbial wisdom to be a resource for Black people in Britain today it is imperative that we have a strong formational and relational role within the Church. In the words often attributed to

St Augustine, 'the Christian faith is more caught than taught'.[26] In what ways as Black people do we seek to influence and inform the wider workings of power within our respective Churches and broader society? How will people 'catch' our relational wisdom of racial justice, inclusivity and good practice in how we live as Black people in Britain?[iv]

This relational challenge to live a life worthy of the calling of Christ, in the power of the Spirit, is summed up in Jesus' summation of the whole of the Deuteronomy code and the Judaic teachings of the law, namely, to love God with all that you possess and to love your neighbours as yourself (Matthew 22.37–39).

Racism, sexism, patriarchy, homophobia, ageism, classism, among other things, all intrinsically deny the love of God because their perpetrators fail to love the wisdom of God that has given them relational opportunities to love their neighbour, often when that neighbour is not like them. 'The beloved community'[27] of which Martin Luther King spoke, and for which he died, is a challenge to cultivate that love of and love for wisdom that connects us with God and with others. It is the wisdom that gives substance to knowledge and that ultimately leads to understanding.

Jesus, the Christ, Black theology and proverbial wisdom

At an earlier point in this chapter I made brief reference to the proverbial qualities of Jesus' sayings – his parables. I now want to argue for repeated attention to be given to how we read these parables, not just as interesting and enlightening stories but also as forms of proverbial wisdom; wise sayings that force us to think again on what

[iv] It needs to be stated that this view is as much *aspirational* as it is *actual*: while Black Christian communities should be centres of racial justice, inclusivity and good practice, based on our experiences or marginalization and oppression, we have often fallen short of this ideal. A combination of poor reading strategies of the Bible, coupled with religious–cultural prejudices have often meant that Black Christian communities and churches can be as exclusive and intolerant as any other institution or body, despite the fact that our historical experiences should enable us to demonstrate better forms of practice. See Anthony G. Reddie, *Black Theology in Transatlantic Dialogue* (New York: Palgrave Macmillan, 2006), pp. 47–82. See also Iva E. Carruthers, Frederick D. Haynes III and Jeremiah A. Wright Jr (eds), *Blow the Trumpet in Zion: Global Vision and Action for the 21st Century Black Church* (Minneapolis: Fortress Press, 2005).

we understand as the truth of God and the kingdom. I want to propose a radical understanding of Jesus who is understood through the complexity of his wise sayings that withstand any easy attempt to interpret them.

By adopting a radical Christology (a radical understanding of the person of Jesus as the Christ) one can begin to construct a new notion of how we learn to live together as one people, one humanity, following the example of Christ. This community is one that operates within the context of a realized and realizing eschatology, which sits in tension with a yet to be realized culmination of God's redemptive purposes for all humankind. That is, through repeated reflections on the wise sayings of Jesus one can assist communities of faithful people to wrestle with the ways in which Jesus' parables offer us ways of seeing the kingdom of God – the kingdom that is now and not yet; the kingdom that is to come, which we are asked to work for and to which we are meant to contribute, in solidarity with God, not knowing when that kingdom will come!

This sense of the kingdom is lived out in community with others, who are also trying to discern what is the truth of the past, present and future existence of themselves and others. This notion of community is one that eradicates the restricted and discriminatory bounded realities in which we presently live, for it does not start from the basis that any one group of persons automatically has more access to the truth of Jesus' teachings than any other. This notion is a radical and profound challenge to accepted wisdom and authority, in which truth and the discernment that gives rise to any truth is best expressed in and through ordained authority figures. Indeed, Paulo Freire has argued that the poor, in spite of their continued oppression, marginalization and denigration at the hands of the rich and powerful, nonetheless have access to forms of wisdom and knowledge that arise through experience.[28] This form of wisdom and knowledge is one that is denied the rich and the powerful, unable to identify with Jesus' own suffering and marginalization which is itself the source of this faithful form of learning that belongs to the poor.

Part of Jesus' critical solidarity with the poor and the marginalized is found in his use of proverbial wisdom that created new forms of knowledge about the human condition and the nature of the kingdom and sought to democratize knowledge. What I mean is that when Jesus used his often complex and confusing stories, he was able to confound the wisdom of the so-called knowledgeable and the powerful. These people were no longer in possession of superior knowledge and therefore deemed to be more powerful.[29] Perhaps it was not only the humbling of the powerful but the fact that his message of justice and righteousness, drawn from the radical prophetic tradition of Judaism, was one that tapped into the experiences of the poor that made Jesus such an attractive proposition for those marginalized on the outer reaches of first-century Judaean society.[30]

A participative Black theology for inter-religious engagement

The notion that Jesus' proverbial wisdom can be a shared and collective means of wrestling with and searching for truth is a proposition that forces us all to reframe what it means to be Black, largely disparaged and without power, or to be White and most commonly with power. And yet the challenges of this proposition go beyond the endemic fault-lines of 'race' between Black and White within the body politic of Christianity. Perhaps one of the bigger challenges that face us as we step tentatively into the twenty-first century is the challenge between the East and the West; between so-called Christian liberal democratic traditions and Islamic theocracy.[31]

Perhaps this radical model of Black theology by means of proverbial wisdom can become a transformative paradigm for an inter-religious process of encountering the self and the other, not only across race or ethnic lines but also across religious ones as well. What would it mean for participants to engage our respective wise sayings (whether cultural or religious or both) across religious lines? How would Muslims engage with Christians? What would it mean for Dalits to wrestle with their respective sayings alongside Brahmins?

This challenge is no mere esoteric or semantic theological abstraction. It can be argued that Black theology's adherence to Christianity, often exemplified in the historic and contemporary practices of the Black majority Churches (chiefly in the USA, South Africa, the Caribbean and the UK), have led it to sail dangerously close to the precipice of religious exclusivity and theological intolerance. On both sides of the Atlantic, Black Christianity in partnership with Black Churches has adhered to a Christian supremacist view of the world by means of an often exclusive Johannine Christology. Through ahistorical and decontextualized readings of John 14.6 (ways of reading that do not take the broader situation into mind), Jesus becomes the only means by which people might be saved. But what happens if this Jesus to whom we swear allegiance, in and through his subversive proverbial wisdom, is beyond the exclusivist, imperialistic labels we try to force upon him?

This particular reading of Jesus, by means of his wise sayings, stands at variance with the Christocentric (Christ-centred) exclusivism of some examples of Black Christianity. We can see this in his 'wise story' of the 'Good Samaritan' (Luke 10.25–37), where the praxis (or righteous action) of the 'Jesus Way' seems to reside within someone who does not renounce his existing belief structures nor claim Jesus as Lord. Rather, it is found in someone who acts in solidarity with those in need.[32] So the person who does the right thing, does not believe the right thing. Now talk about subversive and dangerous proverbial wisdom!

A proverbial, wisdom-based approach to Black theology as a form of inter-ethnic, anti-racist and inter-faith discourse and practice is a process of encountering and engaging with truth alongside others, through and with repeated attention being paid to wise sayings. It is a model of participative Black theology that challenges people to reflect on what they assume as truth and to wrestle with these assumptions and competing notions, while engaging with others.

Perhaps a practical and participative model of Black theology such as this can assist in enabling us to find more creative ways of engaging with the other. This model for encountering self and the other, which is located within an experiential learning exercise, is one that attempts to embody within this educative and learning approach a commitment to multiple truths and alternate and differing perspectives of God and the life we seek to live together and alongside one another.

Perhaps this exercise is one that can enable us to engage in genuine and radical conversation for the sake of racial justice. This is indeed some challenge, and I make no claims for the modest approach found in this chapter – but then again, you have to begin somewhere!

3

Self-discovery: deconstructing Whiteness?

In this chapter I am concerned with how we understand one of the most fundamental dimensions of our overall reality, namely, what does it mean to be human? How do we understand ourselves as people? In what ways are we unique and distinctive and common and yet the same?

The following exercise and the reflections that have arisen from it were first constructed in order to respond to such pressing questions and their effect on Black people across the world. This exercise has been used in acts of worship as a participative approach to enabling congregations to reflect on what it means to be human, and to see how our humanity sits alongside those with whom we seek radical solidarity as members of the one body of Christ. Alternatively, it can be used in any setting where people of faith are enabled to reflect critically on what it means to be human.

Being human!

In one respect, the question of being human can appear to be self-evident, almost an assumed given; namely, that to be human is to be invested and endowed with particular qualities and attributes, capacities and capabilities that constitute what it means to be Homo sapiens. In Christian theological terms, particularly as you read the following pages and perhaps 'perform' the exercise at the heart of this chapter, the major subtext of this work is that of Genesis 1.26, where the Creator declares that humans shall be created in the image and likeness of God. In Christian terms, to be human is somehow, even if only in the faintest of terms, to reflect something of the overwhelming complexity and unfathomable mystery of God. In short, to be human is to be complex and something of a mystery – even to ourselves! As we will see shortly in the exercise that follows, we can construct innumerable ways of defining ourselves as human beings. We can work from clearly observable criteria like gender (male, female) or familial roles (mother, father, son, daughter), to more subjective elements like characteristics (kind, loving, generous, loyal) or passions (a cricket enthusiast, a reader of romantic fiction, a lover of music).

For many Black people, however, defining what it means to be human has been a complex, challenging and quite often painful and painstaking business. Black theology has had to respond to the challenge of what it means to be human. African American Black theologian Dwight Hopkins has undertaken significant work looking at how Christian theologians have sought in their differing ways to understand what it means to be a human being within the context of Christian thought and a belief in the God of the Judaeo-Christian tradition in which Jesus is the Christ.[1]

One of the central points of Hopkins' thesis is that Black religion in its widest sense[i] has always had to respond to the contested nature of what it means to be a Black human being. This contested nature is one that can be seen in the sometimes quoted aphorism of the African American comedian Eddie Murphy. When commenting on the popular 1970s US comedy series *Happy Days*, Murphy is reputed to have said, 'For Black folk there was no happy days in the immediate past. When we go back in time we always end up in chains.'

The truth of Murphy's aphorism lies in the fact that the author of this book is named 'Anthony Reddie'. Reddie is not a name that derives its origins from or in Africa. My familial name is reputed to have come from the west coast of Scotland. My brother, Richard Reddie, was contacted in 2007 (while working on an ecumenical project to mark the bicentenary of the end of slavery) by a White man named 'Reddie' whose family came from the west coast of Scotland and whose ancestors had migrated to the western part of Jamaica, where they had been involved in the slave trade. Our

---

[i] Black religion is often used as a synonym for 'Black Christian faith'. In actual fact the religiosity of Black people extends way beyond the narrow confines of Christianity, but like Hopkins, as a trained Christian theologian, the bulk of my reflections will operate from within a Christian purview. This is not to suggest that Christianity is the only viable religious framework for Black people or, indeed, even the preferable paradigm or model. Rather, it is the framework in which I was socialized and represents the model in which the bulk of Black peoples anchor their spiritualities and relationship to the Divine.

father, Noel Reddie, from whom we have inherited the name, was born and brought up in the parish of Hanover, which is the most western of the parishes of Jamaica. My brother and I have speculated on whether this man is related to us through our paternal links with the Reddies in western Jamaica.[2] When I was growing up in Bradford, West Yorkshire, the people with whom I shared a common or familiar surname (to whom I was not related) were South Asians – Indians to be exact – often called 'Reddi' or 'Reddy'. For many Black people of African Caribbean descent our identities are very complex. For many of 'us' our history is one that incorporates slavery and the experience of forced removal from Africa, followed by oppression and struggle through the long years of colonialism and empire. So even the commonplace facility of being named or owning a name is itself a highly complex and politicized matter.

The continued quest to locate one's sense of what it means to be human is one that confronts all Black people at some point in their lives. The challenge that confronts them is this: In what way does my being Black play any significant part in how I understand myself as a human being? This challenge faces all people of African descent living in the Diaspora – that is, away from the continent of Africa from which our historical ancestry derives.

An exercise in discovering self-identity

The following exercise is essentially a way of exploring how people understand what it means to be human. In what ways are we the same? In what ways are we similar? Again, this exercise is intended as a practical, participative approach to Black theology for the purpose of promoting racial justice, working within the context of Christian ministry and worship. It can be a helpful reflective theological and education tool, even if one chooses not to 'act out' or use it in any practical fashion. It is also something of a diagnostic tool, by which I mean it can be used as a way of helping people to reflect on how they understand themselves.

I would encourage readers to have a go at the exercise themselves and consider how they might define themselves. Indeed, whenever I carry out this exercise I always join in (I have a golden rule of never asking anyone to do something I am not prepared to do myself), and my 'answers' have changed over time and with experience. People are both complex and contradictory, and it is perfectly possible that one can complete this exercise differently depending upon when and in what context one is undertaking it.

Explain to participants that they will be asked to define the different components or elements that make up their identity – the basis of who they are. To do this you will need to provide each with a piece of paper that shows five concentric circles (for an example, see Figure 1). Then ask them to do the following:

- In the innermost circle put down one term that defines you. This term or word is the one that is central to how you see and understand yourself at this precise moment in time. It can be factual (male, female, man, woman) or it can be more a characteristic or a relational term (child of God) or whatever. (Say that you don't want to say too much for fear of giving ideas about what should be put down.) This term is in the innermost circle because it is the most central or important in terms of who you believe yourself to be. (Participants may include two terms, but no more.)
- Be clear that no one can be wrong in this exercise as what you put down is entirely your own choice and is a deeply personal issue about how you understand yourself.
- In the next circle out put down the next two to three terms that you think are central to how you understand yourself. These terms or words are not as central as the one or ones in the innermost circle, but they are still very important. That is why they are in the second circle out. Again, they might be factual terms, personal characteristics, relational terms, faith/theological terms and so on.
- In the next circle out (the third), put down the next three to four terms or words that define you. Again, they are important but not as significant as the ones in the circles further in.
- Repeat this again for the fourth circle out and then finally for the outer circle – the fifth circle.
- What have you put down and where? What is in the innermost circle and why? Ditto with the other terms/words as you move out through the circles.
- Either in pairs or alone, you can look at the different terms/words you have put down. Why are certain words in certain places? What is not there when you compare it with others'? If you are doing this by yourself, you can perform the exercise one day and then

leave it for several days or even let a month pass by (or perhaps longer than that) and then perform it again. Are there significant differences between the two versions? What do the changes say about you and the 'place' you are at when the exercise is undertaken?

- One of the most obvious points to make from the exercise is that we all have multiple selves. Depending upon context, one can place different terms in different circles. If one were to perform this exercise on a number of occasions, it would be possible to have radically different responses, and yet it is still 'you' that is being described by the use of these terms.

Personal reflections

Below I have detailed the terms/words I placed in the five circles on the last occasion I undertook this activity by myself. Reflecting on

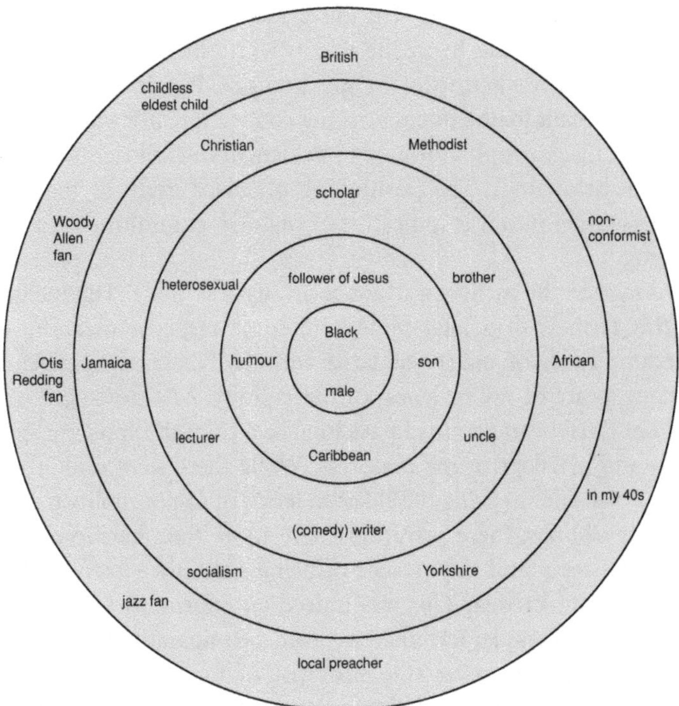

Figure 1 Who am I?

the terms I have used in this exercise it is interesting, but not surprising, that as a Black theologian in Britain I have placed 'Black' right at the centre of my circles, but 'British' is in the outermost circle. So why might that be? Reflecting upon how I construct my own identity, the disparity between where I have placed 'Black' and 'British' is very much indicative of my positive identification with and assertion of one (being Black), but my ambivalence and reluctance to own the other (being British). Many Black people such as myself will describe themselves as African Caribbean. Certainly, one will note the location of the terms Caribbean (second circle out) and African (fourth circle out) as preceding the use of the term British. The descriptor African Caribbean is indicative of my heritage and ethnicity, but tells you nothing about my sense of nationality. It may be instructive to note that as a British-born Black person, *I do not support my country in any national sporting endeavour.* In none of the major sports do I ascribe allegiance to the nation of my birth! In using the term African Caribbean I am identifying myself with the Diasporan African 'roots' and 'routes' (in the British context, both words are pronounced the same, hence the alacrity with which we use such terms as an alliterative heuristic) of my heritage, but in socio-political terms, I remain loathe to confirm my connectionality with a context in which Black people continue to be denied the full rights of socio-cultural belonging.[3] The positioning of 'Black' right at the centre of my self-definition is indicative of my own commitment to Black theology.

Alongside the inclusion of the term Black is 'male'. The inclusion of this term is of a later vintage in some respects, meaning that I became aware of and in solidarity with my Blackness long before I became aware of my maleness or masculinity. As a privileged eldest child of Caribbean parents I have long basked in the apparent invisibility and privilege of my maleness. While there were undoubtedly some downsides to being the eldest in terms of responsibility for one's younger siblings, these privations were more than balanced by the sense of esteem and importance of being not only a 'boy child' but the eldest one at that. This was indeed an enormous privilege, but one of which I was largely unaware until a comparatively recent conversation with my sister (the youngest of four and the only 'girl child'). It was while reminiscing on our schooling in comprehensive schools in Bradford that my sister remarked on the struggle she had experienced following her oldest brother around schools, always being defined in terms of her relationship to me and not in and of herself. She was always identified as 'Anthony's sister' and not as a named person in her own right.

It's often interesting to reflect on what has *not* been stated. When I first began to complete the exercise I was struck by what was not written in my circles: on a number of occasions I had failed to write down 'male'. When I compared my efforts to those of the women in the different groups with whom I was working, very often, if not in all cases, somewhere in one of their inner circles would be some reference to their being women – either in terms of role (wife, daughter) or directly as 'woman' – and for those for whom it applied, often 'Black woman' together. Much later, when reflecting on my different circles, I also realized that nowhere (then) in my circles had I written the term heterosexual.

Reflecting with others

The question of who we are is a sharp one, as illustrated in the following anecdote from when I was leading a session on adult Christian education and theological reflection in North London a few years ago. I was speaking with a group of Black lay people drawn from a number of local churches, and some who did not identify with the Christian faith at all, whether within churches or beyond it. Alongside a preponderance of Black Pentecostals were also a number of Black Anglicans and Catholics, plus some activists from the wider Black communities in London who would describe themselves as being more 'Afrocentric' in perspective.[ii]

For part of the day I was using the circles exercise and asking participants to look at the myriad ways in which they understood themselves as human beings. One Black young man, a 'born-again

[ii] Robert Beckford outlines the two major differing African-centred perspectives on how we see and assess truth in the world. Some see the notion of 'African centredness' as a form of methodology for undertaking a range of academic and scholarly work in areas such as history, cultural studies, theology, sociology and so on. Others will seek a more fundamental appropriation of African belief structures as the basic philosophy that will underpin their whole sense of identity and existence. The former is described by Beckford as 'Afrocentrism' and the latter, all-embracing philosophy, as 'Afrocentricity'. See Robert Beckford, *God and the Gangs* (London: DLT, 2005), pp. 62–71.

Christian' who attended a prominent Black Pentecostal church in London, rose to his feet and stated, 'I stopped being Black when I was saved!'

I have to confess to being aghast at this response. It has never been my approach to tell people definitions or terms with which to define themselves, nor where to place them. The exercise is more of a diagnostic tool: it is used as a way of helping people to reflect on how they understand themselves. What are the many constituent parts of their identity, or should I say identities? My response to the Black people in that particular group was not so much where they put the term Black and how they understood it, as why it should be placed within one of the five concentric circles? Why should 'Black' be acknowledged or not?

The retort from this individual stunned not only me but the other members of the group. Some, like the more militant Afrocentric thinkers, reacted with natural disdain and anger. As the facilitator, it was incumbent upon me to both support and to a certain extent defend the rights of this man to share his view on how he perceived himself. I made it clear, however, that as a Black theologian I was not in agreement with his views. Thus, having shared with the group my belief that 'As you are detailing your own identity, then in a very real sense, you cannot be wrong', that comment was supplemented by, 'You cannot be wrong about how you choose to define yourself. Yes, you can be misguided, or even deluded and in need of therapy and heavy-duty drugs, but strictly speaking, you cannot be wrong!'

What troubled me as I sought to reflect with this individual on his assertion that he had stopped being Black when he was saved was the sense that Blackness was something from which he needed to be removed or even rescued. What was it about the state of being Black that necessitated his being saved from it? I shall say a little more about the complexities of Blackness and Whiteness as ways of talking about or even categorizing humanity in a short while. But I think it worth stating, in as unapologetic a manner as possible, that I see my own Blackness, and that of many others who might so be described, as being a gift of Divine grace that we should celebrate, not seek some form of 'blessed release' from. I am Black because God created me to be so and, like my theological hero James Cone, I see Divine revelation through Blackness and believe God's intent and purposes for redemption, in a world of conspicuous White globalized power, to be revealed authentically through Black suffering and oppression.[4]

I have often asked particular individuals if they have placed certain terms in their circles and if yes, then where? For example, I will ask some of the men present whether they have put 'male' or 'man' down in their inner circles. The responses to this question often vary. What has been interesting are those occasions when certain participants become very impatient, almost angry with me for asking them to acknowledge facets of themselves that they think should remain unstated. For example, on one memorable occasion, when working with an Anglican group, I asked the bishop who was present if he had put down 'male' or 'man'. He said he had not. When I asked him why not, he retorted, 'But surely that doesn't matter? I'm just me!' So I smiled at him, in order to defuse the tension that had suddenly arisen, but then retorted, 'I am somewhat surprised that you think the term male or man has no particular importance, when the last time I checked, the one thing you most certainly needed to be in order to become a bishop was male. I am sure you need other gifts and graces as well, but if you're not a man, then those things are irrelevant. And yet you think it is not important enough to be placed in any of your circles.' He was not best pleased with my response, but the point was made.

At this juncture I am also reminded of a famous retort by a leading African American biblical scholar who, speaking at a Black theology conference in Britain, stunned the audience by remarking that he wanted to develop a 'theology of the penis'! He continued by stating that he wanted to undertake this work because as a man he continued to be amazed that the presence of this organ conferred so much privilege upon him and so many others possessed of this appendage. In many of our Churches, you may not be ordained if you don't have such an organ, and in others, even if you may be ordained, you may not exercise ultimate authority in the Church or be consecrated in the major oversight role as a bishop. To quote my friend, 'I want to know what is so significant in having this thing, because in over 20 years of ministry it hasn't helped me once.' Again, suffice it to say there was a surfeit of embarrassed faces and nervous laughter at this interjection.

Over the many years I have been using the circles exercise, what I have come to realize is that it is often those who define themselves in marginal terms who will seek to put down aspects of their identities that speak to their sense of marginalization. Women will more readily put down 'woman' than men will put down 'male' or 'man'. Similarly, disabled people will often put down their disability while so-called able-bodied people will make no reference to what is their perceived normality. In all the years I have been using this exercise with different people, I have only witnessed one able-bodied person put that term down (or something that equates to it) in one of their circles.

So, as mentioned, in more recent times I have begun to add 'heterosexual' to my circles precisely because it is one of the things I take for granted. It is the normative and taken-for-granted stance of this, and many other facets of our identities that are perceived as 'normal', that is often ignored when people are assessing what constitutes themselves as human beings. And yet it is these very tacit, unstated aspects of ourselves that confer not only supposed normality but often power. It is an uncontested fact that men rule the world. The normality of maleness and masculinity is assumed. One finds it replete within our Christian traditions and in the Bible.[5]

Social theory and Black theology

While I have drawn attention to these different elements of what constitutes our identities, particularly those facets that are often left unstated, what we often fail to recognize is the way in which patterns of knowledge and what we perceive as truth are shaped by particular traditions and theories. Many scholars will talk about socially constructed forms of knowledge that arise from different models of social theory. The term social theory is often used as a way of challenging and interrogating the assumed norms many of us hold in terms of what is understood as 'normal' or 'preferable' or 'right'.

In using the term I am referring to a body of knowledge and philosophical reflections used by scholars in their attempt to analyse and interpret the functional reality of society. Social theory can be grouped into a number of categories. The different branches are linked by a number of characteristics:

1 Problematizing all notions of 'received truths', particularly those that are based on axiomatic, a priori truth claims, such as notions of revelation.

2 Destabilizing any automatic and assumed relationship between language, representation and reality.
3 Contesting and even deconstructing axiomatic and often privileged systems of thought and the accompanying concepts. Black theology has always engaged with some aspects of social theory. In the 'hermeneutical' school[iii] of Black theology, for example, Black theologians have utilized a Marxist critique of history and the workings of power in Western capitalistic societies.[6]

In the overarching development of Black theology, a number of different schools or approaches to the subject have emerged. In the philosophical school, scholars such as Cornel West have utilized Socratic philosophy as a means of undertaking Black theological discourse.[7] In the human sciences school, Robert Beckford, one of the leading Black theologians in Britain, has availed himself of critical cultural theory as a means of undertaking liberative theology from a Black British Pentecostal perspective.[8] All these differing approaches have sought to undertake Black theology while connecting their work to the salient question of 'What does it mean to be a Black human being?' In the philosophical school, Black theologians have argued against a purely Christian theistic basis for talking about Black liberation and freedom.[9] Being human and the desire to accrue the rights and responsibilities endowed to all human persons are not dependent upon notions of divine revelation and the assertion of personhood as defined in authorized sacred texts.[iv]

Whether using Christian-inspired theological frameworks, which represents the hermeneutical school,[10] or in philosophical deduction

---

[iii] The 'hermeneutical' school of Black theology is an approach to the discipline that is essentially Christian in orientation. The term hermeneutics is drawn from the world of biblical studies and can be understood as the art or the science of interpretation; particularly of what one might term sacred texts. This school of thought is one that seeks to locate Black theology from within the Christian tradition. Scholars in the hermeneutical school seek to rethink and reinterpret the meaning of Christian faith and the work of the Church in light of the liberating ministry of Jesus the Christ, which in turn is correlated with the very real existential struggles of Black people.

[iv] At the beginning of this chapter I spoke about constructing a sense of being human with relation to Genesis chapter 1 and the doctrine of creation – namely, that all humanity is created in the image and likeness of God. The philosophical school of Black theology, for example, would not make such a faith-based claim essential in its starting point in talking about what it means to be a human being and the desire for humanity to be free from all that limits its potentiality to be creative, autonomous and self-transcendent.

or using the human or social sciences, Black theology has had, at its heart, a dual focus or concern: first, to challenge the illegitimate use of White power and the construct that is Whiteness; and second, to affirm Black people and uphold the sanctity of Blackness. In terms of the former, Black theology and Black theologians have challenged White people to reflect more critically on what privileges and advantages they accrue from their Whiteness.When I have undertaken this exercise with various participants, only a fraction of the White people in the workshops I have led have acknowledged the significance of their Whiteness in terms of where they have placed it in any of their circles. Most White people when asked have usually failed to acknowledge its significance in a world where being White has marked material, social, cultural and political advantages.

I make this remark fully cognizant of the position a Black man held in the White House in the USA from 2009 to 2017. This statement does not deny the seismic shift that has occurred in the USA with the election of Barack Obama, but one simply needs to juxtapose his excellence with the less than spectacular performance of his successor, Donald Trump, to see the obvious framework of White privilege still in evidence. In effect, Obama had to be singularly brilliant to make it to the White House, at a time, let us not forget, when the USA was in its most parlous state economically in a generation and its stock across the world was at its lowest since the inception of the country in the late eighteenth century. Obama's brilliance can and should be compared to the 'less than average' set of characteristics and skills possessed by his successor. In order to understand the notion of White privilege in terms of the election of Obama one simply needs to pose the question, 'Would a Black person as "average" in intellectual acumen and judgement as Donald Trump *ever make it to the White House*?' When that question can be answered in the affirmative then we will be able to say that Obama's election disproved once and for all the continued presence of White privilege in the body politic of the USA or in other White majority countries in the liberal democratic West.

Critiquing Whiteness

I began this chapter by asking the generic question: 'What does it mean to be a human being?' Then, by way of an experiential exercise,

I have sought to describe how all people have multiple ways of defining themselves. We can complete the exercise in a number of ways and yet the person being described or defined remains the complex and contradictory person that we all know ourselves to be.

Having begun this chapter in a generic sense, I now want to ask a more critical question about one of the most significant elements that is often overlooked or even ignored when this exercise is performed – namely, that of Whiteness or, simply, the term White.

While Black theology has been concerned, primarily, with the need to understand what it means to be Black in relationship to God, the majority of White people in their corresponding theologizing have rarely taken the trouble to understand their Whiteness. In my own work I have used Black theology as a means of challenging White people to reflect on their Christian practice.

One of the ways in which I have used Black theology has been as a means of assisting predominantly White students in theological education to reflect critically on their sense of identities as they attempt to live out their Christian faith under the aegis of racial justice. In this work I have developed a variety of strategies for introducing and assisting predominantly White people to understand Black theology and its contribution to helping them understand their Whiteness and how that can support their sense of solidarity with Black people in the urban context (in which most Black people in Britain live).[11]

The kind of solidarity I have in mind for White people as they seek to work for racial justice alongside their Black compatriots is one that begins from an acknowledgement of the unearned privileges that Whiteness confers. Even when White Christian activists for racial justice are seeking to right and challenge injustice, often from within the framework of urban theology,[v] rarely is it the case that these proponents will have the courage to name their own Whiteness.

White radical racial justice advocates, like their more middle-of-the-road or even conservative peers, are often no more adept at

[v] Urban theology can be defined as the critical reflections on God and faith that are rooted in the personal and collective experiences of, and are drawn from, the concerns arising from ordinary people whose material existence is shaped by and is expressed with what might be understood as an urban context. For a helpful, working definition of urban theology, see Michael Northcott (ed.), *Urban Theology: A Reader* (London: Cassell, 1998), pp. 2–7.

naming their privileged White Eurocentric world. Whereas Black theology in Britain has both named its subjective starting point in assessing what it means to be human (that is, being 'Black', however that is construed, is central to what we often believe ourselves to be), most White British racial-justice activists usually fail even to acknowledge that they are actually White. Acknowledging one's Whiteness is crucial in the struggle for racial justice, for it is in this acknowledgement that one is able to critique oneself, recognizing one's strengths and weaknesses, and so open up oneself to the other.

It is interesting to note that I have yet to see any White racial-justice activist engage in a meaningful fashion with James Perkinson's *White Theology*.[12] The author of this text, a White American, not only engages with Black theology and racism in a critical manner but also seeks to put in the foreground his own presuppositions and socio-cultural and economic position. He does not try to pretend that being White has no impact upon his view of the world or his engagement with others.

From my own perspective as a Black theologian I would like more White racial-justice activists in Britain to pay renewed attention to the basic tenets of the growing field that is 'critical White studies'. This interdisciplinary branch of scholarship has begun the task of naming and unmasking the privileged construct that is Whiteness.

Scholarly work by the likes of Cassidy and Mikulich,[13] Jennifer Harvey,[14] Thandeka[15] and Vron Ware and Les Back[16] would greatly inform the radical action of White racial-justice activists.

Black theology has always incorporated within its semantic gaze a critical dialectic between Black self-determination, affirmation and the construction of its own affective and cognitively derived epistemologies, juxtaposed with the need to mount a robust critique of the specious nature of White supremacy. My hope is that White Christians will continue to support Black people in the committed work of proclaiming the kingdom of God in the urban spaces and culturally plural milieus of this country. For this partnership to work faithfully and fruitfully, White people must be committed to a ruthless and fiercely argued critique of their Whiteness, in a manner that accords with the existential struggling for truth that Black people have been obliged and sometimes forced to undertake since the creation of modernity.[17]

In mounting my critique of Whiteness, it is important that I make the point that this part of this chapter calls for White people to critique their Whiteness as a symbol of supremacy and normality. I am making a clear distinction between Whiteness as a concept of supremacy, superiority and normality (when Black is counterpoised as the direct opposite of these terms) and White people. White people may be prone to collusion with Whiteness and be impacted and affected by its sinful strains,[18] but they are not predetermined to be constrained by it. The liberative Spirit of God in which we are all endowed with free will is one that enables White people to turn away from the privileges of Whiteness (just as men can and should turn away from the privilege of patriarchy and androcentric notions of power[19]) in order to be in solidarity with Black people. White people are not condemned to be imprisoned within the privileged constructs of Whiteness.

The quest for equity, liberation and justice is one that requires the committed, determined action of all peoples, irrespective of faith commitment or none. But it also requires truth-telling and a retreat from all forms of obfuscation that blind us to the structural and systematic, interlocking paradigms that marginalize and oppress millions of people in Britain, of all creeds, ethnicities and cultures.

And yet, amid such complexities, poverty and societal exclusion continue to have a colour. Systemic power, notions of belonging and what is deemed acceptable also have a colour. The failure to name and unmask these forms of unearned privilege and unearned disadvantage has been, for me, the most telling indictment of urban theology in Britain. The days of Black people having to struggle with the pernicious patterns of socio-cultural and religious 'double jeopardy' (we have to solve our own problems and those of White people also, who for the most part have failed to address their own Whiteness) should be at an end.

It is my hope that White people who are committed to racial justice will make greater use of critical White studies as a means of unmasking the privilege construct of Whiteness; for this is not a task for Black theologians alone.[20] Conversely, the task of effecting the systemic and structural changes that better reflect the kingdom of God within the urban context is a task for us all.

The task of proclaiming and living out the values of the kingdom is built upon a radical reassessment and critique of self. In what ways do we understand ourselves? What have we ignored in the process of trying to understand the many components that constitute our identities? What can we learn about ourselves when we attend to the finer points of our many identities, especially those elements we often overlook or even declare to be trivial? It is in the individual and collective reassessment of such matters that we will be better able, as people, to seek to live out the radical collective model of interdependence that lies at the heart of the gospel of Jesus Christ.

4

Reading the Bible with Black theology

The following Bible studies are an attempt to interpret key biblical texts and themes through the lens of Black theology. Each study offers some brief introduction on the historical background and context in which the passage is immersed. The background material is important, for in introducing this to each text I am signalling the relationship between what lies behind the text – the social, cultural, economic and political factors that helped shape the mind of the author, perhaps, in their writing – and what happens in front of the text – the similar concerns of the reader.[1]

In my rereading and interpretation of the texts, I am using a 'Black hermeneutic' as a means of establishing a link between the original context in which they emerged and the more contemporary concerns of marginalized and oppressed people, predominantly Black people of African descent in the early part of the twenty-first century.

Hermeneutics is often understood as the art or the science of interpretation primarily of texts, most often the interpretation of sacred texts, usually the Bible. A Black hermeneutic, then, is the art or science of interpreting biblical texts in light of Black African concerns, which can include Black cultures, experiences, ideas, histories and political ideologies.[2] This approach is informed by Black theological concerns that are attuned to the very real and practical issues of people who can count themselves as marginalized, not only on the grounds of 'race', but also in terms of economics and social and cultural acceptance.[3] The concerns that are central to a Black approach to reinterpreting the Bible are bound up with the differing ways in which one can understand the use of the term Black.

Uncovering a Black presence in the Bible

In the first instance, I am using the term Black in an ethno-cultural sense to mean an identification with predominantly people of

African descent, particularly those who are living in the African Diaspora and are the descendants of enslaved Africans. In this first usage of the term, rereading and interpreting a biblical text using a Black hermeneutic is to seek to establish a relationship between the biblical witness and the contemporary experience of Black people, particularly by finding examples of Black African identity within the text itself.

In the pioneering work of African American biblical scholars we have seen a growing tradition of Black people seeking to enhance the dignity of people of African descent within history by establishing a Black presence within the biblical text as a form of precedence for the importance of Black people in their contemporary time and space. One can cite the work of Cain Hope Felder,[4] Randall Bailey[5] and many others as critical voices in the developing expression of the need to give voice to the hidden Black presence within the biblical text. The importance of this relationship between what happens within the pages of the Bible and the contemporary experiences of Black people lies in the continued belief within Christianity and the societies that have been largely shaped by this most dominant of religious codes that the Bible is a sacred text. If the Bible is a sacred text detailing the ultimate truth of God's ongoing encounter with humankind, then by positing a Black presence within the text one can begin to shape an argument for the validity of Black contributions to humanity by means of our place within the salvation history of the Bible.

One of the important approaches used by Black biblical scholars in their use of Black hermeneutics is their rejection of the pre-eminence of the historical-critical method developed by European scholars during the Enlightenment. The historical-critical method was a means of scientifically excavating the biblical material using the tools of historical study, and was one that put a primacy on human reason and not Church dogmatics as the means of uncovering the often hidden truth contained within biblical texts.[6] Michael Joseph Brown, an African American New Testament scholar, in his reflection on the development of Black hermeneutical approaches to reading the Bible states:

> African American biblical interpretation, even in its academic manifestation, is one such contextual reading. Based on the dual theological

> foundations of liberation and Black theologies, African American biblical interpretation looks for the potentially liberatory reading of biblical texts, the kerygmatic proclamation, behind what otherwise presents itself as a repository of patriarchy, ethno-religious exclusion, and heterosexism.[7]

One of the ironies as I reflect upon the sterling efforts of Black biblical scholars (predominantly African American) to locate a Black presence within the Bible, is the fact that one of the most specious examples of locating an 'alleged' Black presence in the Bible came from White supremacists seeking to justify slavery.

When European traders, particularly in the Elizabethan age, began to engage with Africans on a prolonged basis, mainly through trade, it did not take much imagination to see that the underlying notions of 'otherness' (the marked sense of difference that leads to fear and suspicion) made Black Africans ripe for exploitation.[8] The tensions between religion, faith, ethnicity and nationality are then exploited by means of 'specious' biblical interpretation. The main text that resolved the issue for justifying the enslavement of Africans from within a Christian framework arose from Genesis 9.18–25 – the 'curse of Ham'. Noah punishes his son Ham by cursing his own grandson Canaan (the son of Ham), condemning him and all his descendants to slavery.[9]

Since there was a widely perpetuated belief that Africans/dark-skinned peoples were the descendants of Ham, this so-called 'curse of Ham' was used as 'biblical evidence' that the enslavement of African people was actually willed and sanctioned by God. There was also a similar, fallacious argument based on the biblical story of Cain and Abel (Genesis 4.8–16), where the 'mark of Cain', punishment for the murder of his brother, is interpreted as representing Black skin. Again, people of African origin are somehow identified as cursed by God for some past wrong. Here, any notions of blame are removed from the slave owners since it can be said that the condition in which the Africans find themselves as slaves is due to the sins of their ancestors, for which God is punishing them. Their Black skin is seen as proof of their sinful condition.

Proponents of the Atlantic slave trade constructed such wild and fantastical forms of interpretation of the Bible (in support of slavery) because of the presence of pre-existing views of Africans as 'other' and as being 'cursed by God'.[10] It can also be argued that the profiteering greed of mercantilist-inspired economics was a significant if not an equal motive for the Christian-inspired basis of transatlantic chattel slavery.[11]

The Christianization of enslaved Africans was also influenced by the Haitian revolution at the end of the eighteenth century. The use of primal religions by the enslaved Africans as a source of strength and inspiration, as they fought for their freedom against the colonial powers, made their Christian evangelization a much more urgent task in the eyes of those powers. The charge to Christianize enslaved Africans was also undertaken on a number of biblical and theological grounds, linked to the notions outlined above in terms of Black people being cursed and in need of salvation from the hands of a White, European Judaeo-Christian God.

I think it is important at this point to clear up any possible misunderstanding about the relationship between the very different takes on uncovering a Black presence within the Bible we have so far seen in this chapter. In terms of the attempt of predominantly African American biblical scholars to see and to uncover a Black presence within the Bible, their work has been informed by a detailed historical and archaeological[12] recovery of what has often been concealed knowledge of a Black presence.[13] Commenting on how the likes of Felder and others have sought to recover a Black presence in the Bible, I have stated in the past: 'So far from reinventing a spurious form of counter-hegemony, Felder and others,[14] are asserting both a black presence in and a Black African-centred form of hermeneutics for reading the Bible.'[15] The work of these Black biblical scholars is light years away from the spurious legitimacy of slave apologist exegetes and their attempts to invent a Black presence purely for the purposes of justifying their inhuman and immoral practices.

Identifying with oppression and struggle in the Bible

At the outset, I stated that Black hermeneutical approaches to the Bible were based on two approaches. Thus far, we have investigated the first of the two, namely looking for a Black presence within the biblical text. The second approach starts not with the Black presence in the Bible but the reality of oppression and struggle that has impacted upon Black people in history, particularly during the epoch of slavery. It is this second approach that I have largely deployed in my own work, namely, seeking to connect what exists within the biblical text with the material realities of poor, oppressed Black people within history and seeking to bring the two into a critical conversation.

This approach does not so much look for a literal Black presence in the Scriptures as argue that Black people can identify their struggles and hardships in this world with the Bible by means of reading into the text the themes and concerns that are central to their present existence. Central to this reading is the connection between the biblical text and one's experiences of struggle. This relationship represents the central resource for and the basic thrust of Black theology. Black theology can be defined as: 'the radical re-interpretation of the revelation of God in Christ, in light of the struggles and suffering of Black existence in order that de-humanized and oppressed Black people might see in God the basis for their Liberation'.[16] Black theology begins with the concrete reality of Black suffering and oppression in the world – in the past and the present. It has traditionally reflected upon a number of key biblical and theological themes to guide it in its ongoing development. Three of these themes are:

1 The exodus – God's decisive entering into history in order to liberate God's people from the shackles of bondage and slavery in Egypt.
2 The life and ministry, death and resurrection of Jesus Christ, God's supreme agent for realization of the kingdom of love, justice, peace and reconciliation.
3 Pentecost and the coming of the Holy Spirit that heralds a new dawn for human identity and community living in the form of the newly instituted and ordained Church of Christ.

Central to the theory and practice of Black theology is the belief that the God who is revealed in Jesus Christ is a God of the oppressed. This idea was first developed as an explicit intellectual framework by James H. Cone in his trilogy of early classic books – *Black Theology and Black Power*,[17] *A Black Theology of Liberation*[18] and *God of the Oppressed*.[19]

Some aspects of classic early Christian thought often perceived God as an abstract and distant being who oversaw the creation God brought into being, but whose agency or activity within history was limited to the active intervention in the person of Jesus. God was not only distant and somewhat remote but also neutral. God sanctioned the status quo. So the injustices of slavery were not the concern of God.

The enslaved Africans in the Americas and the Caribbean, through their introduction to Christianity by White slave owners, latched on to the inherent liberative aspects of the Bible, in particular the decisive intervention of God on the side of the oppressed in the Exodus narrative. God demands that Pharaoh 'let my people go'. So God is neither neutral nor distant. The key texts in this respect are Cone's *A Black Theology of Liberation* and *God of the Oppressed.* In both, Cone identifies God with the suffering and humiliation of Black people.

Yet it is important to realize that indigenous peoples of the land, such as Native Americans and Palestinians, will argue that the Exodus is a text of oppression and genocide and not one of liberation. A liberative reading is only possible if one reads the texts from the perspective of the Israelites and not the other peoples who already inhabited the Promised Land.[20]

When Cone asserts that God is Black, he is identifying God with those who are marginalized and oppressed, for whom the term Black has always been linked with negative connotations and demonic imagery. God in Black theology is the active force that overthrows injustice and releases the captors from their oppression. This emphasis upon a seemingly literal invocation of God's presence to mediate the travails of the world and the plight of those who are oppressed continues within contemporary Black religious life. One can see this attempt at convergence in terms of Black hermeneutical readings of the Exodus narrative in the Hebrew Scriptures.

Enslaved Africans latched on to this narrative – the echoes with their slave experience were clearly too obvious to miss. In the Exodus narrative, particularly 5.1–9 and 6.1–9, we can see the cruelty of Pharaoh in his treatment of the enslaved Hebrew people.

In short, by appealing to the biblical text, enslaved Africans were able to redefine the meaning of Christianity from a religion that enslaved them to being one that contained the seeds of their liberation. Exodus was transformed from a specific historical Jewish event in the Old Testament to a more generic and realized paradigm or model for political and social transformation.

There is no substantial record that suggests that enslaved Africans in the Caribbean and the Americas believed that their enslaved Hebrew counterparts in the Exodus narrative were Black. These enslaved Africans were not looking for a Black presence, rather they were searching for convergence. If they could find themes and experiences that echoed their own contemporary experience, and could discern God's acts of liberation within the biblical text, then they could surmise that this same God could do the same for them.

Of course, as present-day Israel shows, the notion of the Promised Land is fraught with dangers for those who may 'inconveniently' occupy the land that has been promised to you by God. In R. S. Sugirtharajah's *Voices from the Margin*, Palestinian Christian theologians often reflect upon the exodus in a negative light.[21] They compare their experiences to those of the Canaanites. The Promised Land means exploitation for some and genocide for others. But for many Diasporan Black Christian people, the exodus remains a powerful theological, political and social ideal. To be in exile in Babylon and to believe in an eschatological hope (the theology of the 'end times') in which you will one day return to a promised land – often a mythologized notion – nevertheless remains a powerful political and social ideal.

I have offered these reflections on Black hermeneutics, looking at the ways Black theology seeks to locate a Black presence within and offers a Black interpretation of biblical texts, as a way of understanding the wider context that informs the following brief biblical reflections.

Short biblical reflections

These reflections use both of the approaches to interpreting the Bible I have outlined above. The purpose of the reflections is two-fold. First, they are offered as examples of how the practice of Black theology can be used to reread and interpret seemingly familiar texts. They show how we can gain new understanding and new perspectives of contemporary life, and the Bible itself, by seeking to use insights from the Black experience as a means of opening up the biblical text. Second, the reflections also invite you, the reader, irrespective of your own ethnic or cultural background, to reflect on how you can use the method I provide as a means of sensitizing yourself and those with whom you may work or engage to see how they can create models of interpreting the biblical text from the perspective of Black theology.

The process and the reflections that followed from it were developed with a group of Black and White Christians in the Birmingham area. The group process I describe helped to create the ideas and concerns that subsequently gave rise to the reflections. The group was taken from three neighbouring churches, and the task was to ask them to choose a number of their favourite passages, following which we would collectively seek to find ways of interpreting them in light of the concerns and themes to be found within Black theology. So the following, in effect, are Black theology-inspired biblical reflections. The passages have been ordered according to their location in the Bible.

The process I employed to assist the group in their approach to interpreting the different passages was as follows:

1 I asked the group to choose a number of passages that they (a) enjoyed reading or (b) that had always intrigued, puzzled or concerned them.
2 As their 'homework', I encouraged them to go to their nearest theological library or church resource centre or Christian bookshop and look at a number of commentaries concerning the passages. The group was encouraged to look at some specialist resources that seek to address the biblical text from a Black perspective or, more generically, from the perspective of those who are marginalized and oppressed.[i] The challenge for the group was to work out if there was a Black perspective or one that resonates with the experience of marginalized people within the text at all. What is the meaning(s) of the text for Black people and others who are oppressed and marginalized?
3 The group was then asked to think of what themes, ideas, concerns or images immediately came to mind when they read the text for the first time. I asked them to record these thoughts on paper.

[i] See Cain Hope Felder (ed.), *The Original African Heritage Study Bible* (Nashville: The James C. Winston Publishing Co., 1993), Fernando F. Segovia and R. S. Sugirtharajah (eds), *A Postcolonial Commentary on the New Testament Writings* (London and New York: T & T Clark, 2007), Curtiss Paul DeYoung, Wilda C. Gafney, Leticia A. Guardiola-Saenz, George 'Tink' Tinker and Frank M. Yamada (eds), *The Peoples' Bible* (Minneapolis: Fortress Press, 2008 and Brian K. Blount (ed.), *True to Our Native Land: An African American New Testament Commentary* (Minneapolis: Fortress Presss, 2007).

4 I collected a number of newspapers, magazines, pictures and other visual images – material that in some way incorporated the views of or was directly about Black people and other peoples who are presently suffering or struggling in the world. Members of the group were also asked to bring similar items with them, for example, a newspaper, a magazine, a picture.
5 The group was invited to link the biblical text in question and their background reading of it (Nos 1 and 2) with the theme, ideas, concerns, images (No. 3), and then link that in turn with **one story** from the contemporary material they had collected (No. 4).
6 The purpose of this (No. 5) was to invite the group to establish a connection between the biblical text and its concerns and a particular concern or context as it pertains to Black people or other groups who might be suffering or in some kind of struggle, as identified in the material they had looked through earlier in the meeting.
7 When the group had explored the interaction between the commentaries on the biblical text, their immediate images, themes, ideas and concerns, alongside the one news item or image, they were then asked to write down ten words or phrases that came to mind. This could be done as a group, or individuals could be asked to put down one word or phrase for themselves.
8 The group was invited (with or without the assistance of a facilitator) to write some short biblical reflections using the words and phrases they had compiled. The reflections were not required to be very long.

The process I have just described was a practical, participative approach to enabling a group of ordinary people to apply the insights of Black theology to their practice of reading and interpreting biblical texts. This approach is one that challenges ordinary people of faith to establish a connection between the sacred text and the real, material concerns of Black people, who are the ones most likely to suffer disproportionately in the world. This process has been informed by the Black theological reflections on the Bible that constituted the first part of this chapter.

In the last part of the chapter I offer some brief biblical reflections that have emerged from the process above. You, the reader, are invited to do a number of things:

1 Having read the process above, you can simply read the following reflections in order to see how the concerns highlighted in the first part of the chapter and the process have given rise to the reflections that follow. If you are working with a group, you can invite them to reflect on the earlier part of the chapter and compare that to the process and see if they can identify the different concerns and approaches in the reflections.
2 If you are working with a group, you can invite them to follow the process I have described, using the same biblical texts found in the following reflections. If you keep the same texts, following the same process, you could then compare and contrast your group's reflections with mine. (It might also be an interesting exercise to ask your group to see if they can guess what images, stories or pictures gleaned from the news media provided the necessary themes that led to my reflections.)
3 Using the reflections as your guide, you can apply the process to some of your own favourite or troublesome texts.[ii]

Isaiah 9.2–7

The people who walked in darkness have seen a great light; those who lived in a land of deep darkness – on them light has shined.

Background

This text is one of the most moving and significant in the entire collection of Old Testament writings. It comes after a dramatic chapter in which Isaiah, a prophet of the Lord, has foretold the impending invasion of Judah by the Assyrians.

The passage has taken on great importance in the many centuries since it was written. For the numerous communities that have been struggling with oppression and social and political marginalization throughout the ages, this text has a special significance.

It speaks of a righteous king who is coming to reign, a king whose reign will be characterized by justice, peace and equality! The fact

---

[ii] The notion of the Bible containing 'troublesome texts' – narratives that have implications for the material and spiritual well-being of those who are marginalized and oppressed – has been explored by R. S. Sugirtharajah. See R. S. Sugirtharajah, *Troublesome Texts: The Bible in Colonial and Contemporary Culture* (Sheffield: Sheffield Phoenix Press, 2008).

that this reign is one that is anticipated in the future has led to two key developments in Christian thought.

Although this passage is Jewish in origin and was written several hundred years before the birth of Jesus, the echoes of Jesus' own birth are very much part of its message for Christians. In short, the future righteous king is none other than Jesus, whose future reign is heralded in this text.

That reign is established only in part through Jesus' birth, which we celebrate at Christmas. Its completion, however, is accomplished in his second coming.

Black theological reflections

Many Black people have experienced slavery, exile, extreme poverty and the continued effects of racism. For them, this sense that 'at the end of time' God in Christ will extend a new reign of justice and peace can be a tantalizing one. It can be likened to an evocative dream. The great African American civil rights leader, Martin Luther King, spoke of his own dream for a new world. This passage today speaks to that dream, a dream for a new world in which all are valued and valuable in the sight of God!

Part of the challenge of trying to live within and for a particular dream is the recognition of when that dream has been achieved. Should our dreams be linked to specific events in history? For example, Martin Luther King dreamt of a time when Black people in the USA would be judged by the content of their character and not by the colour of their skin. Has this been achieved with the election of Barack Obama as President? Does any one event constitute the fulfilment of the dream that King and many others have had, or are these events better understood as many stages towards that fulfilment?

To ponder

- Martin Luther King had a dream. What are your dreams for the future?
- In what ways will your life demonstrate your commitment to making that dream come to fruition?

Jeremiah 31.15–17

There is hope for your future, says the Lord: your children shall come back to their own country.

Background

Many scholars have argued that Jeremiah 30 and 31 were written as standalone texts in order to console a traumatized and grieving people.

Often termed the Book of Consolation, these chapters are believed to have been written as a prophecy for the restoration of the old northern kingdom of Israel, which had been annexed by the Assyrians in the past.

The previous section of Jeremiah 31 concerns the prophecy that tells of a time when those taken in exile will return home. This is a tantalizing vision for the people and we can be sure that this was the intention of the author – to try to bring hope and succour to the lives of the community of which he was a part.

Black theological reflections

There is always an inherent danger in trying to connect ancient sacred texts with contemporary events in that it is too easy to do an injustice either to event or time in history. And yet despite such dangers it would be hard not to connect this text with the many wars taking place across the world today. Many of these are the products of ancient disputes, often arising from the external interference of colonial powers and those who sought to exploit indigenous peoples. One can see this at work in many of the current conflicts in Africa.

One can only imagine the feelings of frustration, anger, pain and separation for those awaiting news and the return of loved ones from war zones across the globe.

The words of the prophet have particular resonance at all times, but particularly as one reflects on significant moments of change, especially when we are moving into a new time or period in our lives, or a new year. *Your children shall come back to their own country*. There must be millions of people all over the world praying that those words come true as they look to the future.

The tension of trying to face the 'new' when we feel there are loved ones who are not alongside us or from whom we are separated, can be almost too hard to bear for many people. The irony for Christianity and for the people who profess faith from within this religious code, is that we speak of the coming of Christ, who is the Prince of

Peace, and yet we have to live within the brokenness of the world in which there is a constant, ongoing denial of the very peace for which Jesus lived and died.

The countless wars and conflicts all over the world, in our present and past ages, and the many millions who have sacrificed their lives in such events, are grim reminders of the capacity of humans to inflict the very worst upon each other – the shedding of sacred blood and the taking of human life.

The promise Jeremiah evokes is fulfilled in Jesus' resurrection and the second coming when he, as the Christ, will reunite the living and the dead. Many Black theologians have pointed to the active visibility of the 'returned', whom we will see once more, as a vindication of the deaths that took them from us in the first place.[22] This is particularly poignant when we remember the countless millions lost to war and conflict and social tumult who never really got to live in their initial lives. What of such individuals, people who merely existed in history but rarely, if ever, lived? The promise and consolation that our children shall come back to their own country is tantalizing, and can entice us like a cheap conjuring trick at a travelling circus. It can hold out the promise of resolution and yet be nothing more than a hollow hope. And yet the promises of Christ are that these things will be realized.

To ponder

- Have you, your family or friends 'lost'[23] anyone recently? In what ways has this loss affected you?
- Imagine Jesus is standing in front of you. What would you say to him about your feelings regarding the person you have lost?

Matthew 1.18–25

She will bear a son, and you are to name him Jesus, for he will save his people from their sins.

Background

This section from the opening chapter of Matthew's Gospel marks the 'run in' to the climax that is Jesus' birth. It follows the opening genealogy of Jesus that serves to establish Jesus' credentials as part of the line of King David. David was understood as God's anointed one in the Jewish or Hebrew Scriptures.

Having established Jesus' relationship with David this passage continues to outline the events leading up to his birth. The story of Jesus' conception, from the engagement of Mary and Joseph through to his birth, is covered in only seven verses.

This highly compressed version of the story (there are no equivalents in either Mark or John's Gospels) does not seek to offer an authoritative historical record of the events of Jesus' birth. Rather, the author's aim is to interpret the meaning of this event in the salvation history of Israel and, ultimately, the whole world.

Black theological reflections

Across the many centuries as people have reflected on this passage, some have taken the 'virgin birth' to mean some form of repulsion at or rejection of the legitimacy of sexual activity. Many Black religious scholars have argued that the nature of Jesus' conception and birth should not be taken as such a rejection. Rather, it should be seen as a means of showing Divine involvement in the emergence of God becoming human and entering into human history.[24] The concern of these scholars is to seek to rehabilitate Black sexuality from the demonized notions of Black people as sexual deviants and lascivious, amoral beasts. These notions have led many Black Christians to adopt extreme holiness codes in which sex and sexual activity are deemed ungodly and abhorrent to God.[25]

The key text line for many people is verse 21 – *She will bear a son, and you are to name him Jesus, for he will save his people from their sins.* Jesus, the saviour of the world – God's special blessed one who is a blessing on the world – enters into our world in order to transform all that has gone before and all that will ever be. Jesus becomes God's supreme agent of hope for the world. The old rules are no more! A new day has dawned! Jesus' presence in the world brings new hope for all oppressed and marginalized people. There is something new in our world that means that all the people who thought they ruled the world are now challenged by a new power, a new reality of justice and peace. This passage is a key resource for Black theologians, for this new son, Jesus the Christ, is the sign of the new age to come, when all forms of oppression and injustice will come to an end. This Jesus is the key sign that God has sided with those who are oppressed and marginalized. God, who is revealed in Jesus the Christ, identifies with the suffering mass of Black people.

To ponder

- Jesus is a blessing to the whole of humanity. In what ways are you a blessing to others? In what ways does your life stand for justice, peace and equity?
- In what ways will Jesus' presence in the world (perhaps in your life) inspire you to break with the old rules and find a new way of being you?

Luke 2.1–20

To you is born this day in the city of David a Saviour, who is the Messiah, the Lord. This will be a sign for you: you will find a child wrapped in bands of cloth and lying in a manger.

Background

This passage is the other birth narrative of Jesus as recorded in the Gospels. In Luke's account, we have shepherds and angels in the story witnessing the birth of Jesus, the Christ.

The text comes after we have witnessed the dramatic events surrounding the birth of John the Baptist. Luke's account offers us a key vantage point of one of the prime witnesses to this story, namely that of the shepherds.

Black theological reflections

The shepherds would have occupied an important social and economic role in the life of ancient near-east communities around the time of Jesus' birth. In rural and agricultural communities, shepherds were hugely important. But their economic importance was not matched by their social status.

In fact as largely nomadic people they would have been on the edge of most communities at this time. People were expected to attend the Temple on a regular basis and observe all the cleansing rituals, but due to the nature of their jobs, shepherds were often unable to attend the Temple and offer the required sacrifice, which necessitated ritual cleansing. So these people are important, the society needs them, but their importance is not matched by their resulting status within the society.

I wonder whether the status of the shepherds might not be likened to sanitation workers in our present time. Most modern societies could not function without these often unseen people who clear away our waste, but they are rarely accorded any sense of social status commensurate with the importance of the job they undertake on our behalf.

In this passage from Luke, the first people to witness the birth of Jesus are, then, a group of persons of low social status. The outsiders get first glimpse of the most amazing event to occur within human history. Talk about having the best seats in the house at an epoch-making event! What a turn-up for the books! But then again, it can be argued that Jesus' birth and continued life has always been one for overturning social conventions and expected norms!

Many Black theologians have argued that the presence of the shepherds in this birth narrative is indicative of the way God is often revealed primarily to those who are the most marginalized and are often considered to be the social outcasts, long before being seen among the powerful and socially accepted. If that is the case, then where are we to look for God's revelation in Christ in our present age? Can it really be the case that God in Christ continues to be revealed in the presence of those who we would prefer not to consider?

Might it not be the case that the lives of poor, exploited Black migrants offer a particular vantage point from which to consider the presence of God in our midst? In many liberal democratic, capitalist societies such as here in the UK, poor Black migrants have a dual role to play within the fabric of the nation. On the one hand, they are scapegoats for vilification and blame by the predominantly right-wing press when it is convenient to cast blame for the ills of the nation; yet on the other hand, we desperately need such persons to do the menial jobs that so-called indigenous people do not want to do.

Given that all forms of capitalism exist on the basis of seeking to maximize profit and keep a hold on wages as a means of doing so, many nations and societies such as this one require poor migrants to work for minimum levels of pay (oftentimes illegally) in order that healthy profits can be made for 'decent law-abiding shareholders'. Perhaps these migrants are the real shepherds of our day. So what if Jesus is to be found among them?

To ponder

- Who are the unseen people of low status whose presence enables our society to function?
- In what ways can the Church, like Jesus, invite these people into the central place of our communities so that they are noticed?

John 1.1–14

In the beginning was the Word, and the Word was with God, and the Word was God. He was in the beginning with God. All things came into being through him, and without him not one thing came into being. What has come into being in him was life, and the life was the light of all people. The light shines in the darkness, and the darkness did not overcome it.

Background

This passage, among the most dramatic in the New Testament, marks the beginning of John's Gospel. This Gospel was the last of the 'official'[26] four pictures of Jesus' life in the New Testament to be written.

The passage essentially maps out the future trajectory or direction of Jesus' ministry and place within the activity of God seeking to save all people. Jesus comes to give life and light to all people – *and the life was the light of all people.*

For many who have suffered from oppression, injustice and marginalization, verse 5 has particular importance. The experience of personal and collective struggle against injustice has often been likened to living within the all-enveloping midst of darkness. And yet, in an echo of the triumphant resurrection, the author asserts that *The light shines in the darkness, and the darkness did not overcome it.*

Black theological reflections

One of the ways in which Black and marginalized peoples have often been tempted to deal with major issues of suffering and death is to seek identification and solace in the death and resurrection of Jesus. The logic goes something like this: if God allowed Jesus, his very own son, to die, not sparing him the agonies of the cross, we should not expect God to spare us.

But given the way in which Jesus' death leads to resurrection and new life for all humanity (the triumph of the cross), then might not our suffering and death be the gateway to new life and the ultimate reward of being transformed beings in Christ? It is a powerful and seductive argument. Writers such as James Cone[27] and Jacquelyn Grant[28] have seen suffering and death as within the overall scope of God's redemptive plans for humankind. That is, God might not purposefully send suffering and death onto God's people (although many actually believe this – after all, isn't that what God has done to Job; isn't suffering simply an example of God's will?); God is, however, in the business of transforming these troubling elements in human experience.

Other scholars, most notably William Jones[29] and more recently Anthony Pinn,[30] have argued that suffering and death can never be redemptive. No form of transformation, learning and resulting new experiences can ever atone for the painful experience, make it less than it was or make it all right or acceptable. Yet many Black people, despite what Jones and Pinn say, still believe in the power of redemptive suffering and transformation.

The news that the light of Jesus Christ is never overcome by the darkness of evil is one that continues to offer light and life to countless millions across the globe. May the light of Christ continue to shine in the hearts of all who are oppressed!

To ponder

- In what ways have you, your family or friends been in 'darkness' in recent times?
- It is often said, 'It is better to light one candle than to curse the dark.' What are the situations, events or people for whom you wish to light a candle now?

John 13.21–35

I give you a new commandment, that you love one another. Just as I have loved you, you also should love one another. By this everyone will know that you are my disciples, if you have love for one another.

Background

This passage, again from John, follows the first half of chapter 13, where Jesus washes the feet of his disciples. In doing so, Jesus is offering his followers a new model of leadership that they are asked to emulate. We then see Jesus informing his disciples that one of them will betray him. The shock of this moment is then replaced by Jesus' command that the disciples love one another. This is the radical nature of the new commandment – that they love one another, even the one who has betrayed them.

Black theological reflections

This new commandment from Jesus sits at the heart of the Christian message and has implications for inside and outside the community of faith.

Inside the faith, the followers of Christ are asked to love another for *By this everyone will know that you are my disciples*. The way in which the followers love one another will be a sign of their commitment to (belonging to), and their actual living, the common life in Christ Jesus.

Sadly, looking back on the events of 2007, a year in which we remembered the bicentenary of the abolition of the slave trade, many descendants of Diasporan Black peoples, the ones who were themselves enslaved Africans, would no doubt have reflected ruefully on this text.

Even when enslaved Africans became Christians, there was little evidence of this love ethic from their often Christian White slave masters. And when many of their descendants migrated to the UK in the 1950s and 1960s, where was the outpouring of love for one another upon their arrival in post-war Britain? *Love one another*. Really?

It is no wonder, then, that many enslaved Africans and, later, their descendants in Britain, questioned the alleged nature of so-called British Christianity. Looking from the outside in, they may have wondered whether many 'good White English Christians' had ever read this passage at all.

At the heart of Black theology, as with many other branches of liberation theology, is the commitment to radical and faithful action (often termed 'praxis') as opposed to mere religious observance. During the era of slavery, it was often so-called White 'saved' Evangelical Christians who were the worst perpetrators of slavery and the chattel confinement of Black African people.[31] For a significant number of 'saved' White people in the seventeenth and eighteenth centuries there was no relationship between the faith they extolled and their actions, in their engagement with people of African descent. Faith was largely a matter of rhetoric, not underpinned by the sort of actions that might give credence to their religious convictions or commend them to others.

In answer to those who might charge me with dealing in gross generalizations, my response would be, 'If my comments are a gross generalization on White people in Europe and America, then explain why this major form of social and cultural evil lasted so long?' In terms of chattel slavery that dealt in Black, African flesh and was used as a major economic buttressing of Western capitalistic expansion, one can chart a trajectory for this evil institution from approximately 1562 through to 1888.[32] Now if the greater majority in Christian Europe and America had felt slavery was such a pernicious evil, one might well have expected the trade to have ended much sooner than it did. One can make similar arguments for the role of ordinary White people in South Africa during the era of apartheid. In these and many other contexts, what one witnesses are the corporate failures to show love to the neighbour. In a previous piece of work I have spoken of a concept I describe as 'contractual compassion', which simply means that those who occupy advantageous and central positions in any society follow the injunction to love the other to the extent to which the other conforms to the image and perception held of them by those with power.[33]

So in effect those who are perceived as the other are judged in terms of their approximation to the values, aesthetics, traditions and so on of the powerful. The closer the other mimics the values and the attributes of the powerful, the more likely they are to be the recipients of Christian love and charity. The greater the difference between them, then the more the converse is true. Maybe that is why many White Christians in the seventeenth and eighteenth centuries, or those in Britain in the 1950s and 60s, were unable to love their Black Christian sisters and brothers (let alone minority ethnic people of other faiths), because they could not love the other that was seemingly so different from them.

To ponder

- In what ways have you failed to love your neighbour as yourself?
- How can the Church inspire people in Britain to *love one another* as Jesus commanded?

Acts 6.1–7

And the twelve called together the whole community of the disciples and said, 'It is not right that we should neglect the word of God in order to wait at tables. Therefore, friends, select from among yourselves seven men of good standing, full of the Spirit and of wisdom, whom we may appoint to this task, while we, for our part, will devote ourselves to prayer and to serving the word.'

Background

This passage follows two chapters where we see the creation and development of the early Church in Jerusalem. Following the outpouring of the Holy Spirit at Pentecost, the early believers, led by the apostles, are creating the common practices for which the Church will be known from this point onwards.

Central to the identity and calling of the Church is the sense that all believers are working for the common good in Christ. This common good includes the sharing of resources (Acts 4.32–37) and here, in chapter 6, the sharing out of the work.

Black theological reflections

This passage has been seen by many as an important source of authority for the development of different orders of ministry in the Church. The disciples seem to be suggesting that they have been given a role that is too important to be wasted on waiting at tables. So they encourage the community to identify a number of other people who can undertake this role.

One of the unfortunate consequences of this text is the belief that seemingly humble and menial roles are the preserve of some and not of others. Many of us have been identified as the ones set apart to undertake the menial work, from which others, who have been destined for 'better things', have been spared.

This division of roles remains a contested one for many from more humble and disadvantaged backgrounds. In what ways are we called to serve Christ, and why does it appear that some people are not destined to have to wait at tables? Didn't Jesus do that for his own disciples at the last supper? One of the issues addressed by Womanist theologians has been the way Black women's bodies have been coerced into serving the needs of male White power and authority.

Delores Williams, an African American Womanist theologian, has spoken of the ways in which Black women's bodies were used as forms of surrogacy by White women during the era of slavery, in order to wean and then rear the children of the latter.[34] Womanist theologians and ethicists have long reminded us of the ways exploitative systems have continued to use Black women as 'convenient beasts of burden' who will do the jobs and menial tasks those in power usually feel are beneath them.

Womanist theology has forced me to consider whether the servant model advocated by Jesus is simply a false and dangerous panacea for those who are the poor, the oppressed and the marginalized, especially Black women. If we believe Jesus to be who the Church has claimed him to be, then as the Son of God his decision to adopt a servant role was his choice. He freely adopted that role and urged his first (predominantly male) followers to do the same. Here we have two problems. First, while Jesus had the choice, the servant model that he advocated was then forced on many poor and oppressed Black people, especially Black women, who did *not* have the choice. Second, the servant model was very selectively invoked, while still wrapped within the framework of privilege and power, which in the end makes the use of the term servant an insult to those who are literally treated as servants. As a Black theologian I am always amused (at best) and insulted (at worst) when I attend ordination services and witness priests and ministers being ordained and then asked to exercise a servant ministry. I wonder what relationship this 'servant' role has to the mass ranks of mainly poor women (many of whom are Black) whose experience of servitude and suffering makes the invocation of this term something of a sick joke.

To ponder

- Do you feel there is an implicit hierarchy in how the Church identifies roles and work to be done in serving God? And if so, does this matter?
- In what ways can the Church affirm the work of all people as they attempt to serve God?

Part 2

Insights from Black theology for sermons

5

Preaching the Bible: is this the kingdom of heaven?

Black theology, in shorthand terms, is the attempt to rethink the meaning of God as revealed in Jesus, who is the Christ, in light of the historical and contemporary struggles and suffering of Black peoples, for the ultimate purposes of liberation. Black theology does not begin with hypothetical speculations on the nature of God or on salvation conceived purely in terms of 'who will go to heaven'. Rather, its focus is on the material and spiritual empowerment of poor, Black oppressed persons in the world, and it seeks to ask in what way the God revealed in the life, death and resurrection of Jesus Christ is in solidarity with the poor and the marginalized as we speak.

Given the importance Black theology places on being alongside and being seen to be in solidarity with the suffering ranks of ordinary Black people, it should come as no surprise that I see the art and the practice of preaching as being a key arena in which the influence of Black theology should be felt. Insights from Black theology can inform preaching and encourage congregations to see familiar texts in a new light. Using Black theology as a lens through which we reread the Bible and reinterpret the meaning of Christian faith can create a framework that enables churches to find more practical ways of being in solidarity with those who are oppressed. This section of the book illustrates how Black theology can become a resource for reimaging the nature and the intent of the sermon within the context of Christian ministry. The following sermons are offered with two aims in mind. First, they demonstrate how I have used the ideas and the concerns of Black theology to interpret a biblical text in light of the material realities and struggles of oppressed Black peoples in the world. This involves looking into the text in light of its historical, socio-political and economic background, as well as analysing how the realities of Black suffering and struggle shape how we read and interpret the text itself.

Second, these sermons, I hope, will also challenge preachers to engage with Black theology as it applies to the congregations and communities with whom they are in contact.

In many respects, the second of the two aims is of greater importance, for it is my hope that this work will inspire others to find ways of both learning from and engaging with Black theology in their ongoing ministry.

In order to assist the reader in seeing how the second aim can be realized in their own preaching ministry, let me furnish a very quick example. Many churches will celebrate harvest festival over the autumn months in their worship services. Members of the congregation will be encouraged to bring produce and gifts to church, and these will be distributed among the needy. The emphasis in many of these services will be on celebrating God's providence, stewardship of God's creation and recognizing the diversity of God's creative masterwork on display in the world. I am not suggesting that there is anything wrong with this focus, but it may not be the only appropriate one.

By adopting a Black theological perspective on harvest, one could also ask critical questions of the ways in which we have read the creation narratives in the book of Genesis, and compare that with the realities of how stewardship of the earth impacts on the poor and those of the global south. Where the Genesis accounts of the creation of the earth state that 'man' is given dominion over the earth, a Black theology account of this text would want to ask critically whether a Western, capitalistic mindset has inferred that the question of power to control and subdue is one that belongs alone to White men with power. Perhaps this is the theological basis of Kipling's famed 'White man's burden'. Perhaps, for certain people in the West, it is their burden to 'civilize' the world and put it under some kind of order – so that others can reap the same benefits 'we' have done within Western, capitalistic, neo-liberal democratic countries.[1]

Certainly, when we observe the workings of the world, particularly in terms of trade, and witness the ways in which many poor, Black people from Africa and the Caribbean, for example, are exploited, a Black-theology perspective on harvest would want to question in what way the refrain, 'And God saw that it was good' is actually true. How do we critically reflect on the biblical and theological images of stewardship and dominion in light of the exploitation of millions of Black people in the world?

Engaging with the ideas of Black theology can inform *all* aspects of preaching, within the context of Christian ministry. How can Black theology influence how we see salvation, the nature of the Church, the practice of Christian discipleship, climate change, immigration and asylum, the minimum wage, the credit crunch? The list is endless.

The following sermon and the one in the next chapter are examples of what can be done, and they are a challenge to those who are preachers to develop their own preaching ministry so that it is informed by the ideas and concerns that are to be found within Black theology. The procedure I outlined in the previous chapter for reflecting on the Bible might assist in this process. I have used it to develop sermons as well as Bible studies and reflections.

The sermon given here as an example was first devised as an exercise.[2] It emerged during the year to mark the bicentenary of the abolition of the slave trade in Britain. During that year I was concerned that there should be theological tools[3] and analysis that would mark the 200-year period since the ending of the trade in Black flesh, alongside the much-needed historical[4] and economic analysis.[5]

This sermon was preached in the chapel at the Queen's Foundation in the autumn of 2007. It has since been used on two further occasions. What was instructive about the previous occasions on which it was used is that each sermon was undertaken without notes. Using the method I have pioneered, namely, an improvised and participative approach to preaching that arises from the use of an exercise or 'interactive games' with the congregation, the sermon is developed from my extemporised reflections on the exercise. The 'text' of the sermon arises from my improvised interaction with the congregation depending upon what has emerged from the exercise itself.

The sermon is offered as an accessible approach to exploring the meaning of Black theology and its relevance for our lives. It is an ingenious and radical approach to reinterpreting the meaning of Christian faith in order to inspire relevant and prophetic models of Christian ministry for the empowerment and liberation of ordinary marginalized and oppressed Black people and other groups who suffer in these conditions.

An example sermon activity: the Parable of the Talents

Opening activity

The text (Matthew 25.14–30 – Parable of the Talents) is read. The congregation is then split into three groups. Group 1 is the first servant, group 2 is the second servant and group 3 is the third servant.

The task then is a simple one (I hope). Imagine that you are one of the three servants (depending upon the group to which you have been assigned) and ask yourselves the question, 'Why do I do what I do?' Why does your character (either servant 1, 2 or 3) act the way he does in the parable?

After a few moments the people in the various groups are asked to respond.

So why do you do what you do?

For some, who are the first servant, you do what you do for a variety of reasons. For some, it is a question of reward. If you work hard, then you know that you will be rewarded by your master. Others will state that the first servant does what he does because it is a tactical move. If you work hard and do what the master desires then he will not only reward you, he will give you greater responsibility and opportunity to progress. So in effect the first servant is using the system as a way of creating space for progress and development within a context or system that is oppressive. We know the system is oppressive because – if you imagine yourself as the first servant – the fact of the matter is that you are a servant. In some commentaries 'servant' can be read as 'slave'. As we will see at a later point in this sermon, the oppressive nature of the context can be seen in the arbitrary actions of the 'master', who has all the power and the freedom to act as he chooses, with potentially dire consequences for those who are at the mercy of his anger and control.

So whether you are a servant or a slave, the fact is that the master has given you his money and expects a decent return on his capital.

You are under pressure and have to make a good decision as to what you will do, because the consequences of a poor decision are not too hard to imagine. One final question I would like to pose to those who are the first servant is: 'Do you love your master?' When I have asked that question on the numerous occasions I have used this exercise, the answer is invariably 'no'. You might respect him. You may even have a grudging admiration for him. But love him? Remember, he is your master. He has power and authority over you, even the power of life and death when it should arise. Come to think of it, that was something of a strange question. In all honesty, it would be quite naïve, dare one say, even foolish, to say that you loved the master.

Now on to the second servant: 'Why do you do what you do?' Again, I can imagine a plethora of responses and a wide variety of reasons. Many reasons may well be similar to those given by the first servant. Fear, expectation of reward, a means of making progress, the possibility of working within the system in order to try and progress. I am sure that some of you will have noticed the prejudicial act of the master at the beginning of this situation, namely, that he gives the first servant more capital than you to begin with. That servant gets more to work with than you. Is that because the first servant is of lighter skin, or speaks with a better accent than you? Clearly, the master is not fair and most certainly looks like he has his favourites. So you might work hard, but that does not mean that you are happy. Why should the first servant get more than you?

So we can surmise that the second servant acts the way he does for a whole variety of reasons, some of which may be about trying to survive, trying to please the master, while among the others might be the desire to create an opportunity for progress within an oppressive and manipulative system.

So on to the final question then! 'Do you love your master?' Once again, this may be seen as an inappropriate or even an insulting question. Why should you love the master? Why would anyone expect you to love someone who has power over you and can control and even exploit you? He is, after all, your master, and you are his servant! He has put you to work and you are expected to 'obey' him and to do his bidding, namely, to make him money so you can make him even richer. The truth is, I guess most of you may come to respect the master, but I doubt most of you will feel inclined to love him.

Finally, on to the third servant. 'Why do you do what you do?' Unlike the previous two, your actions are very different. Not for you the attempt to go out and make the master even richer. No, what do you do? You go and dig a hole and bury his valuable money in a ditch and cover it up. So why do you do that? Why are you so lazy and wicked?

Well, I guess some of you will have noticed that if the master was prejudicial to the second servant in only giving him a fraction of what he gave the first servant by means of capital, then the master really doesn't like or trust *you* at all, because he gives you even less than the second servant. So maybe you start from a position of most definitely not liking the master at all because you know that he thinks less of you than of the other two, or else he would have given you what he gave them.

Whatever the reason, you know that this, your master, is a demanding and selfish person. In fact when he confronts you about your actions, you tell him as much. You tell him that he is a hard-faced crook who takes what isn't his and lives off the rewards of others. You, after all, did not cheat him. You didn't give him back less than he had given you! You gave him back *exactly* the same amount he gave you. But the master is hard and controlling and wants more. So why didn't you do what he wanted? Maybe because you were sick and tired of being used and exploited? Maybe because you had seen how he had dealt with you and the others in the past? So for whatever reason, you decide that you are not going to do your master's bidding. You seek to rebel, to undermine his authority. When he gives you his money to control, you give him back exactly what he gave you, not a penny more and not a penny less!

It goes without saying that you do not love the master. In fact one might even say that perhaps your actions towards him are more honest than those of the other two. For whereas the other two do not give any great indication that they love him, nevertheless they still go along with his wishes and seek to operate within the framework of his expectations and power. But you, the third servant, do not hide your lack of affection for him. Instead, you simply give him back his money and tell him to be happy with it. Well! We all know what happens to you for daring to question the master's authority.

The first two servants are rewarded for their actions, but you, the third, you are punished for your lack of deference to authority. But are you really the villain of the piece as you have been depicted?

Context

I am sure there will be some, if not many of you, who will find some of the assumptions I have read into this story to be unhelpful. How can I say that the master is not fair or that the servants don't love him? Surely, the point of the parable is that the master represents God and the talents are signs and symbols of the master's/God's generosity to humankind? If we use that which God has given us, then we are to be rewarded with more. If we seek to squander the talents/gifts God has given us then the little we have will be taken from us. These, in effect, are the words of verse 29. Those that have, more will be given to them, but those that do not have, even what they have will be taken from them. So let me ask a crucial question at this point. Why do we think the master in this parable is God and why do we think the set-up of this story is representative of the kingdom of God? Is this what the kingdom is really like? Really? So why am I implying that the master is corrupt and that the three servants don't necessarily like him and that maybe the third servant is being the most honest?

If we go back to the text, but reflect on the wider context in which this story is told, we see a number of interesting points on which to think critically.

First, we have to take into account the colonial framework in which this and the whole New Testament was written. The reader should recognize that the context in which much of the New Testament canon was composed was one that echoed to the restrictive strains of colonialism. Judaea, in which Jesus' ministry was largely located, was an occupied colony of the Roman Empire. Scholars such as William R. Hertzog II[6] and Mark Lewis Taylor[7] have shown the extent to which wealth in this province was always connected with economic exploitation.

Second, the Gospel writers are writing at a time when the tentacles of Rome have reached into all aspects of the pie that is the religious and cultural life of the Jewish people in first-century Palestine. We know from history that colonies are exploited for their material resources for the furtherance of the empire in which they are located and of which they are a part. The British Empire's tentacles extended across the Atlantic to the Caribbean, and down to the vast continent of Africa, and many of our ancestors, and indeed some of us ourselves, will know first hand what it means to live on the margins of someone else's power structure. To be a colonized object within an empire is to find oneself an exploited and subjugated presence in one's own country, as that country is being controlled and run for the benefit of and at the dictate of those with power far away from where you are located.

Jesus' message to those first followers of 'the Way' was one that had to speak to the all-enveloping power of Rome on the one hand and the self-serving accommodation and manipulation of this situation by the Jewish religious authorities through their control of the Temple, on the other. As the Indian postcolonial biblical scholar, David Joy, reminds us, those first followers of Jesus were largely landless artisans, ordinary skilled and unskilled labourers without land, economic power or influence in their own country.[8]

These would have been the people at the bottom of the economic ladder who were often excluded from the broader religious and cultural life of the time due to the restrictive purity codes and laws that would also exclude those who were maimed and infirmed. They would have been struggling beneath the weight of foreign and outside oppression in addition to native and internal forms of exploitation. The foreign and outside oppression would emerge from the Roman economic exploitation of the province of Judaea and the need for the Romans to extract material resources from that region in order to service their empire. This exploitation was placed alongside the native or indigenous and internal forms of control exerted by the Jewish religious leaders and the exorbitant rates they charged for enabling the poor to undertake their religious obligations in the Temple. Jesus' anger against the latter can be seen in his overturning of the tables of the money-changers in the Temple – Jesus is angry at the exploitation of the poor as they seek to go about their religious obligations and requirements in God's house. It should be noted that in this text, the term talent refers to a unit of money; in effect, when we read this story in the context in which it was written it seems that we cannot ignore the clear economic and socio-political implications of the parable.

So what are we to make of this parable? If the context in which it was written was an economically exploitative one, then how do we read this story in which the actions of the master seem every bit as manipulative and oppressive as the wider situation? Well, one way of reading this parable is to ignore the material contexts in which it was written and seek, rather, to spiritualize it. That is, this text is not about money, investment and power, but is a metaphor for God's grace and generosity, except that – and this is where even this reading falls down – the master is not very gracious or forgiving! When the third servant does not live up to expectations, he is punished by this very repressive master. Again, I ask the salient question: 'Is this the kingdom of heaven?'

So how do we reconcile the apparent meaning of the parable with the fact that even within it, let alone the wider context in which it was written, we witness the exploitation and marginalization of the poor? Maybe the clue as to how we can and perhaps should interpret this text is to be found in the unwritten attitude of the three servants. Remember the question I asked each 'servant'? 'Do you love your master?' I surmised that none of them did, yet two of the three managed to do what the master wanted, even though there was no deep affection or love attached to the actions. In effect, two of the three managed to disguise their feelings and intent from the master as they went about 'doing their duty'. We shall look at the third servant and his actions in a moment.

If the first two servants were able to disguise their true motives and intent from the master as they went about making him money, then how can we reinterpret this text in light of their approach? What is the meaning of their actions and perhaps that of the whole text?

Signifying

To understand the actions of the first two servants we have to consider a facet of Black life and, indeed, of the lives of all oppressed and marginalized people. This facet or phenomenon is called signifying. Signifying is where, by the use of symbolic speech and actions, one pretends to mean one thing while one's deeper motives and intentions mean the direct opposite. Signifying is where the person seeks to disguise their true motives or intent beneath an outward practice; where, at face value, actions seem to mean something different from the alternative meaning that lies beneath or within what can be seen or heard. Black British theologian and cultural critic Robert Beckford describes signifying as:

> the ways in which African Caribbean cultures 'play', 'manoeuvre' and 'conjure' a subject, issue or event so as to arrive at 'direction through indirection'. Signifying can be a form of trickery that enables oppressed people to negotiate or manipulate the dominant power.[9]

In his description, Beckford outlines the way in which Black (African Caribbean) people have been able to play and manoeuvre a subject or issue so as to achieve a particular objective, but in a manner that is not readily discernible by the dominant power. My interpretation of this text and of the meaning of the parable operates from within a framework of signifying. Let me explain what I mean by this last statement.

When I invited you to imagine that you were one of the three servants in the biblical text, I asked you why you did what you did in the story. You gave a variety of responses. When I then asked if these actions could be understood as denoting any love for your master, most, if not all of you, said 'no'. The truth is, there is no relationship between serving the master as the first two servants do and feeling any sense of love and attachment to that same person. In fact, what would seem to make more sense is that the first two servants are in fact signifying. If we put ourselves into their context and imagine that this story is being told and recorded during an era of colonial exploitation, then it would seem natural that one way in which the oppressed seek to 'make a way' in such a situation is to 'do what you need to do' in order to survive. The fact that the first two servants seek to serve their master could well be seen as nothing more than a convenient tactic in order to seek to survive and make the best of an oppressive and harsh situation.

In fact one would be somewhat surprised to hear, given the realities of this context, that the first two servants would *actually love their master and willingly do his bidding*! If we take the actual socio-economic context of the servants into account, then it seems more likely that they, in their seemingly willing co-operation with the master, were in fact merely signifying, that is, using forms of subterfuge and disguise in order to find a way of making the most of the oppressive and exploitative system in which they found themselves.

The challenge of the third servant is that he or she rejects even the subtle subterfuge of signifying. He or she simply gives back to the master what he was given. The third servant is the one who names the hitherto submerged account of the master's oppressive and exploitative nature. In verses 24 and 25, this servant tells the master what he perceives to be the truth of his actions. He says, 'Master, I knew that you were a harsh man, reaping where you did not sow, and gathering where you did not scatter seed; so I was afraid, and I went and hid your talent in the ground.'

The third servant names that to which the other two fail to give voice – namely, that the master is exploitative and repressive. Why else would the third servant be afraid of him? People are rarely afraid of those in power whom they consider to be benign, kind and generous! We know that what the third servant says must have contained some grain of truth because the master does not dispute the servant's assessment of him. In fact, in the following verse, verse 26, he seems to agree with him, for he says, 'You wicked and lazy slave! You knew, did you, that I reap where I did not sow, and gather where I did not scatter?' You might have thought the master would be affronted and would defend his impugned honour if this was a blatant lie. After all, powerful business moguls have been known to seek recourse in litigation for far milder insults than this!

The master does not contest the third servant's accurate view of him as an exploiter of others. Rather, he simply reminds the servant that if he knew the truth about him, then at least he should have sought to invest his money so that he could get a return on his capital. Isn't it interesting that the master casts the third servant as wicked and lazy simply because he failed to do his master's bidding and make more money for him? For this, even the little he has is taken away from him and he is to be punished severely for his disobedience.

So the moral of the story is, those who do the bidding of an exploitative master and make more money for him will be rewarded, but those who seek to resist outright and refuse to do his bidding will be vilified and the little that was given to them will be taken from them and they will be punished and cast out. But is it? Why have we been taught to see the master as somehow representative of God? What part of God, as represented in the life and practice of Jesus Christ, a man of love and endless charity and compassion, might be represented in this seemingly repressive and nasty piece of work? In fact let me go even further and ask the salient question again. Is this the kingdom of heaven? If this is the kingdom, then God help poor people and those who are marginalized and oppressed. God help those at the bottom of any socio-economic ladder. God help those manipulated into doing the bidding of the wealthy and the powerful. God help those at the mercy of the dictates and whims of their earthly masters, who can punish them and withdraw what they have given to the poor if they even dare to behave outside the confines of the regulatory framework that circumscribes these, the least of these.

By the way, it is worth noting that the parable that follows this one is that of the Sheep and Goats, where the basis on which the punishment or eternal judgement meted out to those who did not show charity to the oppressed is that they ignored the material needs of those who were deemed the 'least of these'. Can this following parable (Matthew 25.31–46) be read as a challenge to the actions of the master in Matthew 25.14–30?

Whatever we make of that later parable in Matthew, what we can say about *this* one is that taking the economic, material realities of the text into account, then the poor and the marginalized are not beloved by God. Far from having a special or preferential option for the poor, as liberation theologians such as Gustavo Gutiérrez[10] have asserted, it would appear that God has a preferential option for the powerful and the oppressors. If this parable is indicative of the kingdom of heaven, then maybe God will not help the poor. For in all truth, if you are exploited and shafted on earth, then the kingdom of heaven will not be any better!

A Black theology rereading of this text

The scenario outlined in this text is not a fanciful one. The set-up of an exploitative master who seeks to make money out of his servants or slaves is not a work of ancient near-east fantasy. Rather, this set-up speaks to the very real historical experiences of Diasporan African peoples and our struggles for full life throughout the epochs of slavery and then colonialism. There are many echoes between this first-century picture of exploitation within the Roman Empire of the landless Jewish artisans of Galilee in Judaea (what David Joy calls the 'subalterns'), and the exploited and subjugated bodies of enslaved Africans during the British Empire, first during slavery and then during colonialism.

In both contexts, the simple overriding question is, how do you survive? How do you make a way in an exploitative and dehumanizing system that is designed to rob you of choices and any sense of autonomy and human dignity?

Black theology as a form of theological inquiry, as well as a framework for the practical, prophetic expression of the Christian faith in word and action, arises from the lived reality of being Black in a world of rampant exploitation and oppression of Black people. Black theology begins with Black people's reflections on the nature of their marginalization and oppression in the world. While there are a number of Black people who can display a sense of success in the world, for the most part Black people in many of the richer countries of the world, not forgetting those in the poorer ones, are condemned to live their lives on the receiving end of oppression and exploitation.

When you were asked to inhabit the characters of the three servants in this biblical text, that was an opportunity to go beyond the spiritualized ways in which the reading and interpretation of these stories have often been taught and into one that asks you to live the reality of the people at the centre of this narrative. When the real, lived realities of these characters are placed alongside the historical experience of Black peoples, and then interpreted in light of these experiences, suddenly a new interpretation of the text emerges. Black theology is a form of Christian-inspired reflection on the ways in which life should be lived under the guidance and sustenance of God, for the purposes of full life and liberation for those who are exploited and oppressed. It is informed by those who have been and continue to be exploited and cheated of their full rights, reflecting on the realities of their marginalization and using that as a means to reinterpret the basic meaning of the Christian faith.

When Black people, and others who have suffered a similar (but not the same) fate of being exploited and controlled by those with power, have used their experiences to reinterpret biblical texts and rethink Christian tradition and orthodoxy, then new forms of thinking, leading to potentially new forms of action, can emerge.

This can be seen if we directly reinterpret this text in light of the very real suffering and exploitation faced by Black people during the era of slavery and then later during British colonial rule. For enslaved African people in the Caribbean islands during the seventeenth and eighteenth centuries, life was controlled and regulated by White slave masters. Enslaved Africans were denied any major sense of individuality or autonomy. Rather, they were treated purely as objective things as opposed to human subjects, whose only function was for economic profit. All were forced to work for their masters for the economic betterment of those masters.

In such contexts, how could one survive? Some, often identified by the term house negroes – those given more responsibility by the White masters to work within 'Buckra's house' (the name of the slave master's house) – might seek to use their position as a means of doing the master's will in order to survive and to make a way out of no way. For many working in 'Massa's house', this was akin to the first two servants making the best of a bad situation. The fact that they seem to be doing the master's will should not be confused with any sense that they were either condoning or seeking to justify the system. Just as many of you who adopted the identity of the first two servants could do the master's bidding but still have a sense of injustice and grievance about the overall situation, then so too could the enslaved Africans living in 'Buckra's house'.

Now this is not to say that all the enslaved Africans living in the big house rebelled, but neither does it mean that their seemingly willing co-operation should be read as agreement. For many, their actions in being seen to go along with the dictates of the master should be understood as a form of what I described above as signifying – engaging in symbolic speech and action in order to survive within an inhospitable situation by pretending to feel one thing while often thinking and feeling another.

But alongside the house negroes, the ones living in Buckra's house, we also have to reflect on those who were the 'field negroes', those banished to the outer reaches of the slave master's estate, working hard in the sun in order that the master might make his profit. For many of these, their form of resistance was one of outright rebellion. It is one of downing tools and saying to the master, 'Look, we know you are an exploitative crook, and we are not going to do your bidding any more.'

It does not take much imagination to work out the reaction of the slave master to such insubordination. Mutilation and death! The slave master's reaction may not have been that different from the master in the text when confronted with the insubordination of the third servant.

If we take a Black theology approach to reinterpreting this text, our answer to the salient question, 'Is this the kingdom of heaven?' must be a resounding 'no'. If we think back to the context in which Jesus tells this story, we will remember that it was during a period of colonization. Many of Jesus' first followers would have known at first hand the realities of economic exploitation and oppression. So Jesus' message of good news and liberation had to speak to the material realities of their existence. How do you survive in this corrupt world? How do you live when all around you, rich and powerful people, are using you and exploiting you? How do you resist without using violence or turning into the mirror image of the people who are oppressing you?

In this text we see Jesus engaging in a process of signifying. Jesus, speaking right under the very noses of the Roman power brokers and the corrupt and repressive Jewish Temple authorities, is painting a picture that all of those first hearers would have clearly recognized. This parable is not a picture of the kingdom of heaven. On the contrary, Jesus is signifying. He is saying that this is the world as you and I experience it. This is the opposite of the kingdom of heaven! *In effect, the kingdom of heaven is not like this!*

Jesus, in offering us three characters in this parable, is showing his first hearers, and all people in every oppressive and exploitative context, options for how to resist. For some, their resistance will be one of seeking to make the most of the corrupt and unfair situation in which they find themselves. It is one of being 'wise as serpents but innocent as doves' (Matthew 10.16). But for others, resistance will be of a more militant fashion, one that refuses to give in to the master's exploitative dictates. But as the parable illustrates so clearly, taking this route will lead to the ultimate penalty – banishment into 'outer darkness' (Matthew 25.30).

The good news for us today, as we read this text, the good news for all oppressed, marginalized people, whether Black or those who are women, are disabled, are poor, gay, lesbian or transgendered, for all these people, the good news is: *This is not the kingdom of heaven.*

6

Preaching theology: rethinking original sin

Right from the outset, Black theology, like all theologies of liberation, began by questioning the claims of orthodoxy and the acceptance of traditional Christian doctrines. Black theologians have challenged some of the so-called fundamentals of the Christian faith, arguing that these were either misunderstood or that our adherence to them had negative consequences for oppressed Black people.

In many respects, the development of Womanist theology in the 1980s pressed the case even more strongly for a challenging of the central ground of Christianity by those who are marginalized and oppressed in the world. In Chapter 4, on reading the Bible, I utilized some of the thinking of Womanist theologians and ethicists in order to critique the servant motif within Christianity.

Perhaps the most startling departure from Christian orthodoxy within Black and Womanist theology can be found in the work of the African American scholar Delores Williams. Williams argues that Jesus' crucifixion should not be understood as redemptive or salvific but rather seen for what it was: a brutal execution, undertaken by the machinations of a corrupt state, of a righteous person who sought solidarity with the poor and marginalized. She argues that to make the cross a means of salvation is to glorify violence, which can then be used as a means of convincing the poor and marginalized (disproportionately women) that suffering should not be resisted, for it is indeed redemptive.[i]

[i] One of Delores Williams' central arguments is that the cross itself is not redemptive, rather it is Jesus' life, his teachings and his ethical examples that give life. She argues that Jesus in effect did not die for our sins; instead, he died because of them. That is, in being in full solidarity with the poor and marginalized and seeking to empower them to ask critical questions of the status quo, Jesus was crucified – a political prisoner's death – as a consequence of his radical revolutionary actions. So his death has social and political underpinnings and not just spiritual ones. See Delores S. Williams, *Sisters in the Wilderness: The Challenge of Womanist God-Talk* (Maryknoll: Orbis, 1993).

Black and Womanist theologians begin with the realities of Black suffering, marginalization and oppression in the world as their basis for talking about God. Using Black experience as their starting place, as opposed to the strictures of doctrine and tradition, this leads Black theologians to depart from many of the traditional ways of understanding the meaning of the Christian faith. Black theology places the primacy on the reality of the Black experience and not on the Bible or Christian tradition or Church history. James Cone emphasizes this point when he writes:

> To put it simply, Black Theology knows no authority more binding than the experience of oppression itself. This alone must be the ultimate authority in religious matters. Concretely, this means that Black Theology is not prepared to accept any doctrine of God, man, Christ or Scripture which contradicts the black demand for freedom now. It believes that any religious idea which exalts black dignity and creates a restless drive for freedom must be affirmed. All ideas which are opposed to the struggle for black self-determination or are irrelevant to it must be rejected as the work of the Antichrist.[1]

For Cone, Jesus' resurrection on the third day is a physical, historical event, not because the dictates of Church authority and orthodoxy have decreed it thus, but because he sees the Gospel accounts as resonating with his belief in a liberating God. If the claims for a liberating God in Christ who will overcome the negative forces of evil and oppression are to hold weight for oppressed Black people, then this event has to be something more than a mere symbolic remembrance in the minds of Jesus' first followers.[2]

The sermon that follows is my attempt to use the method of Black theology (beginning with the reality of the Black experience of suffering and oppression in the world) as a means of rethinking the traditional understanding of original sin in Christian theology. It demonstrates how Black theology, with its emphasis upon real, material analysis of human experience in history and its impact upon Black life and struggle, takes precedence over theological rhetoric and the application of universal, seemingly generic Christian doctrine. These factors shape how the word of God is rethought and not the other way around!

The sermon is a Black theology reinterpretation of one of John Wesley's 44 sermons. Wesley preached thousands of sermons in his long life, but these 44 sermons have become an almost alternative canon (in supplement of the Bible) for Methodists, alongside his notes on the New Testament. It is still a requirement of all lay preachers that they should be conversant with Wesley's 44 sermons as a whole, and they are consequently examined on one of them at a final oral examination and testimony before their peers in their local preachers' meeting.[3] My sermon was originally written at the invitation of the Revd Dr Angela Shier-Jones.[4] I had been invited to submit a sermon for a collaborative project looking at how contemporary Methodist preachers reflect on Wesley's foundational 44 sermons. Due to sheer carelessness I did not respond to the invitation until all the more 'enticing' of Wesley's sermons had been taken. I found that only a handful of the 44 sermons remained on which I might write a contemporary sermon.

The editor insisted that each contributor should submit a genuine sermon and not some scholarly essay masquerading as one. That is, the written piece should be something we would actually preach or imagine preaching. As someone whose preaching has always been essentially improvised and extemporized,[5] the challenge of writing out a full sermon that was not a scholarly essay in disguise was very real.

As in the previous chapter, the sermon in this chapter is an invitation not only to see how Black theology can inform preaching, but also a challenge for those of you who are preachers to see how the concerns and ideas of Black theology might inform the sermons you preach. How can Black theology challenge accepted orthodoxy, not for its own sake, but rather for the purposes of enabling the poor and marginalized to see the God revealed in Jesus Christ as one who is wholeheartedly on their side and is God of justice, righteousness and liberation?

An example sermon[6]

It has to be said that the notion of 'sin' is one that has fallen out of popular parlance of late. The old image of the sober-suited preacher, usually resplendent in dour, dark, serious colours venting his spleen at 'we miserable sinners who have all fallen short of the glory of God' is one that is in short supply. There are many people, I am sure, who will decry the lack of teaching about sin in general and original sin in particular as being one of the main reasons for the alarming drop-off in church attendance in Britain or the lack of moral fibre among our callow youth.

I retain, still, a distant memory of sitting in a Methodist church in my youth, in West Yorkshire, at a badly attended and dour evening service where the local preacher, a very serious-looking, white-haired, elderly man regaled us all on the sinfulness of our generation and the reason why many of us were going to go to hell if we did not repent immediately and give our lives to the Lord. I remember one memorable sentence when he charged us to consider the fate of our mortal souls as we made our way home through the winter gloom of that evening.

'What would happen', he charged, now clearly warming to his task, 'if you were to be hit by a bus on your way home and should die not in a state of grace with our Lord and Father? What would happen to you then?' I can assure you that this sermon certainly concentrated our minds and gained our immediate attention. When the organist then chimed up with, 'Just as I am without one plea' and the preacher made the resultant altar call, a number of the young people, myself included, all dashed headlong to the front to save ourselves from the impending fiery furnace of hell. Just to ensure that I would not be snatched downstairs through the trapdoor, so to speak, I decided that I would take the longer route home that night, which took me away from the busier streets and all oncoming buses. Well, you can't be too careful now, can you? Better safe than sorry!

Original sin, the notion that human beings are fallen creatures due to our disobedience to God, and as such are flawed and distorted beings in need of redemption and salvation from God, is one that lies at the heart of Christian thinking. While it might not get a regular airing in many pulpits in the contemporary era, there is no doubting its continued pervasiveness in Christian teaching and interpretation. For after all, many of our Churches, indeed my own Church, will still talk about Jesus Christ as the ultimate means of grace, and preach that salvation is to be found in him. Salvation, the act of being saved, implies that one is being saved from something, while also being saved into or for some other purpose or place.

To be saved from something also implies that there is some situation or position in which the person is located or stuck in order to necessitate their needing to be saved. This brings us back to the notion of original sin. Human beings need saving because we are sinful, and a righteous and holy God, a perfect God without stain or fault, cannot coexist with sin. Hence the saving work of Jesus.

As I have stated already, even if we do not hear too many direct references to original sin there is a sense that it still permeates the basic fabric of the Christianity so many of us practise and proclaim in our lives.

So what is it about original sin? What are we to make of it? Is it really necessary, or indeed does it have anything to say to us in the contemporary era?

First, let me get in an apology! As I often tell people whenever I preach these days, I am a Black liberation theologian, so don't be surprised if I say things that will upset you; after all, that's my job. Now, I could explain to you what I mean when I use the term Black liberation theologian, but to be honest with you it would take too long and such explanations would not accomplish a great deal. So what I will say is this: I am paid to break the rules. Black theologians by definition do their own thing and are not confined by the frameworks of the conventional, the powerful or the polite. As I am neither conventional, powerful nor polite, you may get the drift of what is coming next. It is not pleasant, and some of you of a nervous disposition may wish to look away now.

As a Black liberation theologian I take a dim view of the traditional notion of original sin. John Wesley's 38th sermon in his now legendary 44-sermon series makes it clear that original sin is an integral part of the human condition. Human beings are inherently sinful. However we read the Genesis narrative of Adam and Eve and creation, whether literally, as pre-history or as an allegory or symbolic interpretation of an essential but complex truth, there is nonetheless the clear sense that human beings messed up, and that they messed up big-time.

The sin, originating out of human pride and a conceited and ill-advised sense of our autonomy, is one that has cosmic dimensions. It is one that holds for all time and across spaces and all contexts. In effect, all of us are born guilty of sin and of being estranged from God.

This separation from God finds echoes in numerous passages in Scripture. Psalm 51.5 reads, 'Indeed, I was born guilty, a sinner when my mother conceived me.' And Romans 3.23 reads, 'all have sinned and fall short of the glory of God.' Cheerful stuff, huh? No wonder so many of us flocked to the front of that church to get the reassuring moist hand of salvation clasped onto our head at the end of that service all those years ago!

Wesley may have believed in the efficacy and reality of original sin, but I do not; or at least, as we shall see shortly, if there is a sense of its existence, then I have a radically alternative take on its essential meaning. But first, why am I at odds with Mr Wesley, given that I am one of his lay preachers for good or ill? Well, my problem with the notion of original sin lies in its general disregard for context or the particular nature of human life as it is lived in certain contexts and times and places in history. Like much that can be understood as Christian theology, there has always been the tendency to go for the universal and the generalized, as if there really is a way in which we can make irreducible and deductive truths fashioned from philosophy and theology that hold for all people at all time. As a Black theologian I simply do not hold this view to be true. Not of original sin, nor of any other so-called theological truth or doctrine that has been conceived by the Church.

In response to my last piece of rhetorical bombast, some might cry foul and shout, 'Heretic'; 'Call yourself Christian?' Well, they wouldn't be the first to think that. But not to worry, I have a fast car parked outside, with the engine running and a formula-one driver at the wheel ready to whisk me off and away from the mob baying for my blood. Not very likely, if we are honest. The English don't go in for conspicuous shows of emotion. More like the limp handshake at the end of the service and the damning words of indifference – 'Thank you, that was *nice*.'

But I digress. So what is it about original sin that does not chime with me? Well, in the face of real and demonstrative human suffering and evil, original sin says that we are all guilty and sinful. In classical terms, to quote one of my old and beloved Sunday-School teachers, 'Anthony, sin is sin. Whether you get 1 per cent or 99.9 per cent, if the pass mark is 100 per cent, then you've still failed.' Only godly people who have confessed their sins will go to heaven and not merely the good ones who tried to be good.

I never believed that version, even when I was told it as a child. It doesn't make any sense in terms of the reality of life as it is lived and experienced by some. We are all guilty. Really?

Wesley, in his sermon on original sin, talks about universal wickedness. His reference to this phrase arises as he reflects on the life of human beings before the great flood. He says of that time, 'The universal state of affairs was evil, complete and utter wickedness, quite unrelieved by any good.' Dire stuff! Wesley, like many contemporary Christians, sees sin as an abstract universal failing of humankind and one for which the only remedy is Jesus.

Many people, particularly those who have lived through and experienced great suffering and oppression in their lives, have asked questions about the universal notion of sin. So we are all equally sinful and in need of saving, are we? There is no real difference between people in their basic orientation, as all of us are below the high and impossibly exacting standards of God. Really?

I did warn you that I am a Black theologian by conviction and training! Well, a friend and colleague of mine, Professor Anthony Pinn, who is an African American Black theologian in the USA, has challenged much of the commonly accepted notion of original sin in some of his recent work. In his most famous book, *Why, Lord?: Sin and Suffering in Black Theology*, Pinn argues against the classical teachings of Christianity particularly as they relate to sin, suffering and oppression. He asserts that the reality of the latter, namely, oppression, in his case of African Americans, especially during the era of slavery, makes the notion of the former, the idea that *all people are guilty of sin*, even those who suffer immense hardship, a very bitter pill for some people to swallow. Pinn wonders what sin the tortured and disfigured Black body swinging from a rope in the Deep South, having first been flailed and lynched, committed to deserve being labelled a sinner?

Similarly, within the British context and of a more contemporary nature, when Black Caribbean people came to Britain and were confronted with wholesale racism and rejection from good White Christian folk, I am sure it was very, very cold comfort to be told that they were as sinful as the people who were despising and rejecting them. Or what about the parents of Stephen Lawrence or Anthony Walker, two Black young men killed before their lives had barely begun because of the colour of their skin, due to the still all too latent attitudes of White supremacist thought and Black unacceptability in this country? What were they guilty of? Were they equally as sinful as the ones who murdered them? For we are all under judgement, due to original sin, aren't we? Were they condemned to judgement by the mere and unspecific accident of simply being born human?

The concept of original sin has simply no means of engaging with the specific, cultural and historical settings in which evil and suffering take place among people of specific ethnicities and backgrounds. Many Jewish theologians have long since jettisoned any sense of acceptability of the Christian view of atonement, redemption and forgiveness at the hands of a God who seems utterly powerless to bring justice for the poor, the oppressed and suffering in this lifetime. The Holocaust has cast doubt upon the relevance, let alone the theological efficacy of original sin.

For many Black Christians who have endured their own forms of suffering and marginalization, not only is God seemingly powerless to change their situation in this life, but they are then told that access to the next life is based upon acknowledging their own innate faults and failings, while others, including this same God, seem unwilling to take seriously their pain and struggle in the here and now.

Speaking as a Black theologian in the contemporary world situation where over 30,000 African children will die while my own government can spend billions on a war most of the British public did not want, at the behest of a former leader who claimed to be acting on the dictates of his own Christian conscience, I can see why William R. Jones uttered the plaintive cry, 'Is God a White Racist?' Jones, an African American post-Christian theologian, wondered what was the point of God for suffering Black people. Either God could relieve their suffering but chose not to, in which case God was a sadist, or could not actually change their situation, in which case God was impotent and not worth believing in.

In either case, the idea that these suffering people are innately sinful just like everyone else seems not only to add insult to painful and despairing injury, but I would go further and call this type of theological construction a sick joke. Perhaps Jones was right, in that while Christianity is often content with speaking into an abstract contextless vacuum of universal sin, Black people die in their millions. Maybe God does love White people more than Blacks – after all, did not Katrina and Tsunami demonstrate the essential truth that natural disasters have a particular liking for killing and devastating the lives of darker-skinned peoples? Maybe Jones was right and God is a White racist.

Now, I can see a number of you looking somewhat underwhelmed by depression and despair! I was told by my first local preacher's tutor that you should always leave the congregation with the good news of Christ! I can sense some of you ruminating, saying, 'And you call this good news, Mr Preacher?' Well, I have to confess that thus far it has been a tad less than joyful. A bit depressing if truth be told! But then again, when was sin ever meant to be cheerful or fun? But I take the point!

So what am I saying? Well, I reject the traditional notions of original sin. I reject good Mr Wesley's notion of original sin. But I do admit to humans possessing the capacity to besmirch the Godness and the goodness within us. This is what I understand to be sin, whether it is original or simply a cheap imitation – only time will tell! This capacity is not a cosmic one or one that transcends history or specific encounters in the lives of particular communities or groups in certain times and spaces. Rather, this view is one that holds to the separation between one human being and other humans, a separation in which God is not seen. It is one that anchors sin in the concrete and the material, within specific situations and contexts that take seriously that some people are most definitely more guilty than others, although ultimately we are all guilty of something, no matter how fleeting that thing might be.

From a Liberationist theological position, sin is invariably seen differently from what is often the case in traditional Christianity. Speaking as a Black theologian, I do not doubt the reality of sin in human affairs, both recent and historic. The truth is, as people we all possess and actually engage in thoughts and actions that are contrary to God's holy will and are therefore sinful.

I want to offer us another way of thinking about sin in general and original sin in particular, one that moves us away from the spiritualized and overly generalized model that has been bequeathed to us by our spiritual fathers and mothers, good Mr Wesley included.

Like Wesley, I want to go back to Genesis for a clue as to the nature of God's call on humankind – a call that has always possessed a dual focus, one later summed up in Deuteronomy 6.5 and Matthew 22.37–39, namely to love God with our heart, soul, mind and strength and to love our neighbours as ourselves. I will return to the Matthew passage in a short while, for it provides the basis of my understanding of the reality of sin in the context of this address.

In the creation narratives or stories in Genesis, God creates humans in God's own image. Men and women are created to be companions for one another and to live in that partnership under the sovereign rule of God. In the many narratives of the Old Testament that follow on from this creation account in Genesis, we see this framework played out again and again.

The life of obedience and faith that God asks of the people he has set apart, the children of Israel, whose stories and experience we see recounted in what we call the Old Testament, is one of a constant battle between trying to follow God, and the selfishness and a form of 'insider's culture' preventing them from being the selfless, inclusive and God-centred people they were called to be. We can see this tension in many ways, throughout the Old and New Testaments. In the famous account of the Tower of Babel (Genesis 11) we see a cautionary tale of arrogance and the human vanity that seeks an alleged autonomy. I believe that this passage is not a rebuke to humankind and its vanity, but rather is a challenge for all communities to accept that their attempts to monopolize and colonize God for their own purposes are always doomed to fail.

When we attempt to parade our own alleged superiority as the will of God, and try to ignore the needs or the legitimate rights of others, then God's justice emerges in order to show us that corrupt and selfish forms of power that masquerade as allegiance to God will not be tolerated. Black people know at first hand what it means to be on the receiving end of powers and principalities that seek to disguise their evil intent by wrapping themselves in the alleged word of God. As we remember 1807 and the act to abolish the slave trade in Britain, we are reminded of the selfishness and greed that caused one set of people to believe that they were created in the image of God more than their neighbours, and to believe that they could pervert God's word to suit their own materialistic economic ends.

Original sin is not the spiritual breach between God and humans. I believe God to be infinitely more flexible and engaging with humankind than the early Church Fathers or John Wesley could ever have understood. The God many of us worship is big enough and loving enough to take on board all our failures, individual and collective. Rather, original sin is that which runs contrary to God's imposition to love one another as we love God's very own self.

In Matthew 22.37–39, when Jesus is asked a typically challenging and politically fraught question by a Pharisee – What is the most important commandment? – Jesus' answer is clear. He returns to Deuteronomy 6, namely, loving God with all that we possess. But there is an interesting sting in the tail, for Jesus knows that loving an invisible God who has no graven images can be an illusory task. For how do we see God? How do we discern what it is to love God? If God can't be seen or felt in a direct way, then how do we love God? It can be all too easy to love a sometimes silent and elusive God, but still hate the people you can see. White Christian slave owners loved God, but still despised and oppressed their fellow human beings who just happened to be Black. Good African Christians belonging to one tribe no doubt loved God, but still managed to commit genocide on their fellow African neighbours simply because they belonged to another tribe.

History is littered with the sin of self-centred regard and lack of care, love and solidarity for the other. So Jesus ensures that such abstractions as loving a God you cannot see, and this being the sole basis of Christian practice, is overturned and can no longer be so easily invoked. Now it is no longer sufficient to love God, with all one's heart, soul, mind and strength, in isolation from the need to love one's neighbour as oneself. The second part of the clause comes into effect. We are called to love our neighbour as a way of showing our love to God. Now it becomes something of a challenge to effect this love of God, for in having to love the very real and embodied presence of the neighbour, we can suddenly see that this love makes crucial demands upon us.

Unlike the conventional notion of original sin in which it is hard to discern any serious ethical or pastoral charge one could make to those who oppress others and those who are oppressed as, after all, we are equally guilty of falling below the exalted standards of God, now we have a more concrete and specific sense of sin. For sin is that which separates us not from God, but rather from each other. When one person or group seeks to limit or even obliterate the God-ness or the goodness in the other we are not only doing it to God's own self (Matthew 25.31–46), we are also violating God's covenant with all humankind in Christ. For Christ came that all might have life and have that life in all its fullness (John 10.10).

Sin is now no longer abstract and universal, but concrete and specific to all times and spaces. We can see what this sin looks like. When a rich, largely White federal government in the richest country in the world fails to attend to some of its poorest citizens during a natural disaster in the form of hurricane and resultant flood, and those people happen to be Black, then it has sinned against its neighbour and, in so doing, against God who is reflected in the lives of those poor and dispossessed peoples. When immigration laws in a so-called civilized nation, which claims to be a Christian country influenced by ancient Judaeo-Christian values, find convenient ways to let rich White Europeans in but condemn poor people of all colours to exclusion, then that country too has committed a sin against its neighbour and, in so doing, against God who is reflected in the lives of those poor and dispossessed peoples.

So you see, although I do not subscribe to Wesley's notion of original sin and have no great regard for its unworkable formulations in a world of rampant economic exploitation, racism, sexism and homophobia, I do believe there is a very real presence of sin in the world. That this sin might be described as 'original' may well be discerned in the desire of the first human communities to attempt to please themselves and take delight in their warped sense of autonomy rather than depend upon God's providence and the desire to live in mutuality and partnership with the other. Whether that sin is indeed original at all, or just ongoing cheap imitation of tawdry capitalistic values and the basic greed that has always stalked the world throughout history, is a question for scholars far cleverer than me.

May God so touch our hearts, through Christ and in the power of the Holy Spirit, that we as individuals and communities of faith might be enabled to move beyond the desire to look after the 'us', whoever the 'us' might be, and not to live in solidarity and love with the 'other', whoever they might be and wherever they are located.

Concluding thoughts

This sermon has sought to rethink the meaning of sin (in general and original sin in particular) by reinterpreting it through the focusing lens of Black theology. This process of rethinking has not been undertaken for its own sake, as an example of Black theologians trying to prove themselves as clever as their White counterparts. Rather, the process of changing the meaning of orthodox doctrine is for the purpose of affirming and empowering marginalized and oppressed Black people, indeed all people who are presently suffering in the world. In the specific context of this sermon it is to remove the absurdity of those whose reality is one of exploitation and suffering being assessed as in the same category of 'sinfulness' as those exploiting them.[7] Many Black theologians (this one included) have too many recent memories of being told by White, imperial Christianity that they are *as sinful, in the same way*, as those who are exploiting and oppressing them. As you have seen from this sermon, I am not arguing that Black people and others who are oppressed are without sin or are incapable of sinning; it is just that the basis of what constitutes sin is to be reframed. This reframing is meant to take account of the existential realities of life for those who are oppressed, rather than work out a formula that is based on religious mythology and takes no account of context, issues of power, social location or culture.

Taking my cue from Womanist theologians, in this sermon I have sought to demonstrate what happens to our hitherto accepted norms when we subject them to the very potent realities and experiences of those who are marginalized and oppressed.[8] Jacquelyn Grant, in her groundbreaking Womanist theology text from the late 1980s, shows the extent to which seemingly 'neutral', 'objective' and 'normative' Christian theological formulas are nothing of the sort. She argues that in effect much that is constructed as objective and normative in Christian doctrine is in fact subjective speculation informed by the White middle-class patriarchal views of its authors.[9]

For far too long, Christian orthodoxy has been dominated by the perspectives of the educated elite and has failed to be informed by and made to meet the needs of those who are Black, poor, marginalized and oppressed. My challenge to all preachers and those engaged in other aspects of Christian ministry, irrespective of ethnicity, culture or class, is to subject their theological reflections to the material realities of those whose experience of life is one of unremitting pain, suffering and hardship.

Afterword
Black Lives Matter!

During the years since this book was first published, I have been struck by how little has changed. As I write this, I am reflecting on the resurgence of the Black Lives Matter movement. In writing this piece against the backdrop of the upsurge in direct action led mostly by young people across the world, and as I reflect on why, to so many people, Black lives do *not* matter, I am forced to look at my own life.

The writer of this book is an African Caribbean male, who is now in his mid fifties, but was in his mid forties when this work began. I was born in Bradford, West Yorkshire, to Jamaican parents who came to this country from the Caribbean in the late 1950s. As such, I am a second-generation Black African Caribbean British subject. I was born into and nurtured within the Christian faith from the Wesleyan Methodist tradition. I ply my trade as a Black liberation theologian and decolonial educator working within Oxford University, but have been domiciled in Birmingham since 1987.

Growing up in Bradford in the 1970s and 1980s occurred against a backdrop of racism and economic deprivation. Our family lived in one of the poorest areas of the city, in a clean, tidy and respectable home, which nonetheless came with no central heating and had an outdoor toilet or 'privy' as it was called. The evangelical Methodist church in which I was nurtured in the faith was supportive, but nothing they said or did in that church spoke to the social location and experience of being a first-generation Black British-born person. The truth was, they did not need to say anything, because the normative Whiteness of the Church blinded them to the realities of racism within the church and the wider city.

To be clear, the members of my church were kind and gracious people, but they had nothing to say to the persistent reality of racism that affected the lives of all non-White people in the city of Bradford.

I would argue, the consistent and persistent challenge that has faced Black Christians in Britain has been one of trying to get White Christianity to give expression to an anti-racist articulation of the gospel. In using the term 'White Christianity', I am talking about people of European extraction and descent, who form the majority of the population, who believe in the God revealed in Jesus Christ and give expression to the central tenets of the Christian faith in myriad forms of social-cultural practices.

White Christianity was oblivious to our realities and social existence. Worse than that, this church and many others were complicit in the racism we experienced as disenfranchised Black bodies living in Britain. I remember, in the late 1970s, a march by White Christians seeking to 'win back the city for Christ'. I remember many of the leaders in the church I went to speaking excitedly about the need to participate in this event. The growing influx of Muslims from the Indian subcontinent was the catalyst for the march. Despite the evangelical zeal of my mother, the spiritual anchor of the Reddie family, she knew better than to advocate that our Christian family take part in a march that owed more to a desire to shore up White privilege than it did to restating the supremacy of Jesus Christ as the Lord of the city. Instinctively, we all knew that, although we were card-carrying members of the church, this march was not for us!

This afterword seeks to remind us that the Black Lives Matter movement has had a long period of gestation, and from long before the death of George Floyd there has existed a history of ideas and practices that have rendered Black lives of limited importance – indeed, often of no importance at all.

I offer these reflections for three reasons. First, we need to remind ourselves that systemic racism predates George Floyd's death by a long way. Second, as heinous as George Floyd's death was, we need to recognize that most Black people do not experience the same extreme level of police violence. Rather, what we face is a litany of often covert forms of racism that are not as visible and dramatic as what happened on that day. The racism that many of us experience is systemic in nature, often hidden in 'plain sight', which the COVID-19 pandemic has revealed as being more than just our paranoia or having 'chips on our shoulders'. Third, we need to understand that the disregard directed at Black bodies is based on centuries of toxic theological ideas, which means that a radical, liberatory Christian response must be something more than simply quoting biblical texts, such as Galatians 3.28 or Revelation 7.9.

Backdrop to the Black Lives Matter Movement

The existence of racism in the UK today, and in many parts of the so-called developed West, is testament to the continuance of an underlying Eurocentric, Judaeo-Christian framework that has invariably caricatured Africans as 'less than' and 'the other'. The notion that human beings can be categorized by a fixed set of identities that determine their human potential and capability, often expressed in terms of morality and ethics, can be traced back to the first four centuries of the Common Era (CE).[1] It was during this epoch that negative connotations pertaining to Black people as the 'other' began to surface in Christian thinking.[2]

The scourge of racism in the UK is thus nothing new for Black people. Whatever COVID-19 has revealed in terms of social and economic disparities between Black and White, these have their roots in history. As Robert Beckford has demonstrated, one can chart a genealogy of racism in European intellectual thought that has exerted a disproportionately negative hold on the life experiences of Black people.[3] Scholars, such as Eze, have shown the extent to which the allegedly enlightened thinking of such philosophers as Hume and Kant was infected by White supremacist thought.[4] The construction of the binary of Blackness (as bestial and 'less than') and Whiteness (as the personification of goodness and opposite of Blackness) is a product of modernity.[5]

The chief legacy of transatlantic slavery was the unleashing of the rampageous and ravenous animal that is racism. The construction of racialized notions of Black inferiority and restricted perspectives on Black humanity was the dangerous offspring of the chattel slavery of the 'Black' Atlantic.[6] The outworking of an unchanging and hierarchical manipulation of humanity did not disappear when the Act to abolish the British slave trade was passed in 1807. The Act brought the making of slaves to an end but racism, the notion of White supremacist norms, most certainly did not end. And so today, having witnessed at first hand the White flight from inner-city churches in the UK, along with the anti-immigration rhetoric of those in favour of Brexit, we need to remember that the antipathy expressed by many ordinary, seemingly respectable White people to the presence of Black bodies has had a long incubation period.

Toppling the monuments to White supremacy!

The Black Lives Matter movement emerged to counter the patently obvious fact that, throughout the so-called 'developed' world, Black lives do not matter. This is not just a question of economics or materiality; it is also about seemingly intangible matters, such as the impact of racism on our psyche and associated questions of representation and spirituality. It has been interesting to observe the concern of some White people for matters of law and order and governance and property in relation to the tearing down of the Colston statue in Bristol. I worked for a year in Bristol and was confronted with the sight of statues built in honour of men who enslaved my ancestors. Polite petitions to move these and other statues were ignored. Long before a group of protestors tore this one down, Black activists asked for it and other statues to be moved to museums where those who wanted to see them could, while saving those of us who didn't the ignominy of having the lives of our oppressed ancestors constantly insulted. White authority ignored our voices. To them *our lives don't matter* and, in the face of White complacency and disregard, *our feelings don't matter either*.

In 2007, I campaigned, along with many others, for a national monument to mark the epoch of the slave trade and the countless millions who died under the yoke of British slavery. We were peaceful, respectful and went through the time-honoured democratic channels, and successive governments ignored our entreaties. So why should we be surprised that, following the pulling down of the Colston statue, we heard the anguished voices of White people airing their greater concern for property than for the feelings of Black people? Why is it that White people can complain about our not abiding by the rules when our attempts to do so have been ignored completely and treated with indifference and contempt? At the time of writing, the Prime Minister can promise swift justice for those who 'desecrate' public statues such as that of Colston in Bristol, but cannot do so for the members of the Windrush Generation deported under the previous Tory administration, or for the disproportionate numbers of Black people who died in the Grenfell Tower disaster.

The Black Lives Matter movement presents the Church with one of the most significant ethical challenges to have confronted the Body of Christ in our times. The challenge for White Christians is to live out the gospel imperative of solidarity with Black people, and to recognize and strengthen the bonds of love through our shared faith in Jesus Christ. Even when Black people became Christians, there was little evidence of this love to be found in the actions of many White Christians.[7] When many Black people travelled to the UK in the post-war migration of the 1950s and 1960s, where was the outpouring of Christian love for one another on their arrival?[8]

White English Christianity must commit to a radical and ruthless critique of its Whiteness, in a manner that recognizes the basic life struggles for meaning that Black people have been obliged, and sometimes forced, to undertake. In critiquing Whiteness, I am talking about a thorough deconstruction of the toxic relationship between Christianity, empire and notions of White-British superiority.[9] And one tangible expression of this deconstruction of the past will be the refutation and rejection of the so-called glories of empire and the legacy of the likes of Edward Colston, for whom many are still pining.[10]

If Britain wishes to demonstrate its commitment to Black Lives Matter and erase the historic stains of empire and colonialism, which set the very template for Black bodies being viewed as inferior within the economy of White supremacy, then we must finally have a serious conversation about reparations. The biblical and theological case is a strong one, if we accept that God is not colour-blind and cares about racial injustice. The consequences of the sin of White supremacy,[11] about which Christian theology has long been silent, need to be reversed and this can be symbolized and realized in material terms through a process of reparations.

In Jesus' two great commandments – to love the Lord your God and love your neighbour as yourself (Matthew 22.37–39) – we see the significance of holding in tension the need to give honour to God while remaining in right relationship with other people. You cannot love God without loving and showing justice to your neighbour. It was the reformers of the sixteenth century who, in their anxiety to downplay or even remove 'works of the law' as a means of salvation, diminished the interpersonal dimension in their understanding of the Christian life. For them, to be saved largely meant that people needed to believe the right thing, without necessarily acting in ways that might express the ethical imperatives resulting from their faith in Jesus Christ. This separation of the ethical connection between faith and works led to the likes of Edward Colston being elevated as a pillar of the Anglican establishment in Bristol. Until comparatively recently, the Church of England still provided a service to mark the beneficence of this great philanthropist – who also just happened to be a notorious slave trader![12]

If we reflect on the disparities between 'God's economy' and the exploitative economies of empire, thinking especially of the savageness and greed of Edward Colston's slave-trading activities, it becomes clear how much we need alternative theological frameworks for attesting to what we might call 'God's righteousness'. Scholars such William R. Hertzog II[13] have shown the extent to which wealth in occupied provinces such as first-century Judea was always connected with economic exploitation. So, when Jesus challenges the 'rich young ruler' (Mark 10.17–27 NKJV; Matthew 19.16–22 NKJV) to give away all he has and follow him, he says this in the knowledge that the young man's wealth was not amassed in a neutral context. Both the rich young ruler and those who first heard what Jesus said to him would have known why Jesus, in effect, tells him to make reparations by giving his money to the poor.

Today, the impact of the Black Lives Matter movement around the world alerts us to the problems and injustices inherent in the global economic order. The present world economy operates like a modern empire, in which the White power of the Global North and West exploits and perpetuates the comparative powerlessness of Black and Brown people of the Global South and East. As with the story of Jesus and the rich young ruler in the Gospels, Jesus' encounter with Zacchaeus (Luke 19.1–11) reveals how an ethic of restorative justice can be a means of effecting reconciliation between exploited and exploiter. Today, the Zacchaeus Tax Campaign (organized by Church Action for Tax Justice) and the New International Financial and Economic Architecture (NIFEA) initiative are examples of practical theological work that advocates a form of restorative justice within the world economy.[14]

The use of finance for constructive purposes is a liberatory theological and ethical commitment that demonstrates Black Lives Matter. It is a reminder that money, when used for just purposes, can be a means of grace. At the same time, the need to examine and address the greed and exploitative nature of White global capitalism has been given even greater impetus by the grim statistics for the disproportionate deaths of Black people from coronavirus during the pandemic. For Black lives to *really* matter, we need to address the underlying societal and economic disparities that have led to disproportionately more Black people dying from COVID-19 than White people. This pandemic has not been a 'great leveller, but a revealer'.[15]

The push for reparations for Black people[16] is based on the understanding that we need to pursue forms of restorative justice. And the need for reparation is one that all must recognize if Black Lives Matter is to mean something more than the mere rhetoric of finely written statements.

God – who is not colour-blind – demands nothing less!

Notes

Introduction

1 For further details on this, see Anthony G. Reddie, *Black Theology in Transatlantic Dialogue* (New York: Palgrave Macmillan, 2006), Michael N. Jagessar and Anthony G. Reddie (eds), *Postcolonial Black British Theology* (Peterborough: Epworth, 2007) and Michael N. Jagessar and Anthony G. Reddie (eds), *Black Theology in Britain: A Reader* (London: Equinox, 2007).

2 See James H. Cone, *Black Theology and Black Power* (20th anniversary edition, New York: HarperSanFrancisco, 1989).

3 See James H. Cone, *A Black Theology of Liberation* (20th anniversary edition, New York: Orbis, 1990).

4 See James H. Cone, *God of the Oppressed* (New York: Seabury Press, 1975).

5 For a very good discussion on the use of the term 'Black' as a means of describing people of African descent, see Algernon Austin, *Achieving Blackness* (New York: New York University Press, 2006).

6 See Centre for Contemporary Cultural Studies, *The Empire Strikes Back: Race and Racism in 70s Britain* (London: Routledge, 1982).

7 See Michael N. Jagessar and Anthony G. Reddie (eds), *Postcolonial Black British Theology* (Peterborough: Epworth Press, 2007), pp. xiii–xv.

8 For an excellent treatment on the presence of Christ through the elements of bread and wine, see Dennis E. Smith, *From Symposium to Eucharist: The Banquet in the Early Christian World* (Minneapolis: Fortress Press, 2003).

9 For a discussion on Jesus being Black and what this means for Black theology, see James H. Evans, Jr, *We Have Been Believers: An African American Systematic Theology* (Minneapolis: Fortress Press, 1992), pp. 86–7.

10 See Cone, *God of the Oppressed.*

11 See Jacquelyn Grant, *White Women's Christ and Black Women's Jesus* (Atlanta: Scholar's Press, 1989).

12 See Robert Beckford, *Dread and Pentecostal: A Political Theology for the Black Church in Britain* (London: SPCK, 2000).

13 See Jagessar and Reddie (eds), *Postcolonial Black British Theology.*

14 See Paul Ballard and John Pritchard, *Practical Theology in Action: Christian Thinking in the Service of the Church and Society* (London: SPCK, 1996).

15 See Duncan B. Forrester, *Truthful Action: Explorations in Practical Theology* (Edinburgh: T & T Clark, 2000).

16 Elaine L. Graham, *Transforming Practice: Pastoral Theology in an Age of Uncertainty* (Eugene: Wipf and Stock, 2002).

17 Jeff Astley, Leslie J. Francis and Colin Crowder (eds), *Theological Perspectives on Christian Formation* (Leominster; Grand Rapids: Gracewing; Eerdmans, 1996), p. x.

18 Jeff Astley, *The Philosophy of Christian Religious Education* (Birmingham, Alabama: Religious Education Press, 1994).

19 This term is borrowed from the comparatively recent Anglican-led, but ecumenical report looking at the role of faith (in general) and churches (in particular) as conduits for social change and transformation in urban contexts in Britain. See *Faithful Cities: A Call for Celebration, Vision and Justice* (London: Church House Publishing and Methodist Publishing House, 2005).

20 See Anthony G. Reddie, *Acting in Solidarity: Reflections in Critical Christianity* (London: DLT, 2005), pp. xvii–xxii. For a more technical assessment of what I am terming 'performative action', see also Jose Irizarry, 'The Religious Educator as Cultural Spec-Actor: Researching Self in Intercultural Pedagogy', *Religious Education* [*The Vocation of the Religious Educator*] (Vol. 98, No. 3, Summer 2003), pp. 365–81. See also Clark C. Apt, *Serious Games* (New York: Viking Press, 1970).

21 Extensive examples of this work can be found in the following, all by Anthony G. Reddie: *Acting in Solidarity: Reflections in Critical Christianity* (London: DLT, 2005); *Dramatizing Theologies: A Participative Approach to Black God-Talk* (London: Equinox, 2006); *Black Theology in Transatlantic Dialogue* (New York: Palgrave Macmillan, 2006); *Working Against the Grain: Re-imaging Black Theology in the 21st Century* (London: Equinox, 2008).

22 See Reddie, *Acting in Solidarity* and *Dramatizing Theologies.*

23 See Dwight N. Hopkins, *Introducing Black Theology of Liberation* (Maryknoll: Orbis, 1999), pp. 1–13.

24 For further details, see Emmanuel C. Eze, *Race and the Enlightenment* (Oxford: Blackwell, 1997). See also Dwight N. Hopkins, *Being Human* (Minneapolis: Fortress Press, 2005).

25 For two helpful resources for engaging in racial justice work, see Sandra Ackroyd, Marjorie Lewis-Cooper and Naboth Muchopa, *Strangers No More: Transformation Through Racial Justice* (London: the Methodist Church, 2001) and Sandra Ackroyd, Marjorie Lewis-Cooper and Naboth Muchopa, *Workers for the Harvest: A Process for Equipping Racial Justice Facilitators* (London: the Methodist Church, 2005). For a helpful analysis of the different forms in which racism is manifested, see also Naboth Muchopa, *Making a Positive Difference* (London: the Methodist Church, 2001).

26 This DVD is entitled *The History of Racism* (in three parts), and was broadcast (for the only time as I write) in March 2007 to mark the bicentenary

of the abolition of the slave trade act in 1807. Part 1 deals with the long gestation in the development of 'race' from classical antiquity to the 'Middle Ages'. Part 2 looks at the practice of racism when linked to chattel slavery during the epoch of the transatlantic slave trade, and Part 3 starts with the abolition of slavery in the USA in 1865 and ends at the present day.

27 The renowned Black British documentary film maker, Robert Beckford, has outlined this ongoing development or 'genealogy' of racism from the era of slavery through to our more modern times. See Beckford, *Dread and Pentecostal*, pp. 67–94.

28 This is described in greater detail in Anthony G. Reddie, *Nobodies to Somebodies: A Practical Theology for Education and Liberation* (Peterborough: Epworth Press, 2003) and *Dramatizing Theologies.*

29 James Cone argues against the notion of a passionless, neutral and indifferent God in one of his classic early texts. See James H. Cone, *A Black Theology of Liberation* (Maryknoll: Orbis, 1990), pp. 1–20.

30 Cone, *A Black Theology of Liberation*, pp. 17–20.

1 Affirming difference

1 This is part of my formal title in my work, which is based at the Queen's Foundation for Ecumenical Theological Education, funded primarily by the Methodist Church of Great Britain.

2 This issue is addressed by Robert Beckford in the first ground-breaking Black theology text in Britain. See Robert Beckford, *Jesus is Dread: Black Theology and Black Culture in Britain* (London: DLT, 1998), pp. 96–111.

3 See Charles R. Foster and Fred Smith, *Black Religious Experience: Conversations on Double Consciousness and the Work of Grant Shockley* (Nashville: Abingdon, 2003), pp. 15–43.

4 See Anthony G. Reddie, *Nobodies to Somebodies: A Practical Theology for Education and Liberation* (Peterborough: Epworth Press, 2003), pp. 95–6.

5 See Dwight N. Hopkins, Lois Ann Lorentzen, Eduardo Mendieta and David Batstone (eds), *Religions/Globalizations: Theories and Cases* (Durham and London: Duke University Press, 2001), pp. 7–32.

6 See Frantz Fanon, *Black Skin, White Masks* (London: Pluto Press, 1986).

7 Josiah U. Young, 'Envisioning the Son of Man', *Black Theology: An International Journal* (Vol. 2, No. 1, Jan. 2004), pp. 11–17.

8 See Reddie, *Nobodies to Somebodies*, pp. 132–40.

9 Lorraine Dixon, 'A Reflection on Black Identity and Belonging in the Context of the Anglican Church in England: A Way Forward', *Black Theology in Britain: A Journal of Contextual Praxis* (Issue 4, 2000), pp. 22–37.

10 The African American Black theologian Dwight Hopkins addresses the question of diversity in his reading of the kingdom of God in one of his

more recent books. See Dwight N. Hopkins, *Being Human: Race, Culture and Religion* (Minneapolis: Fortress Press, 2005), pp. 53–80.

11 Robert Beckford, *Dread and Pentecostalism* (London: DLT, 2000), pp. 193–6.

12 Anne H. Pinn and Anthony B. Pinn, *Black Church History* (Minneapolis: Fortress Press, 2002), pp. 35–8.

13 One can cite scholars such as Edward Blyden, an early advocate of the need for Black people in the African Diaspora to look back to Africa as a means of enabling them to feel a greater sense of pride in their God-given Blackness. See Edward Blyden, 'Africa's Service to the World: Discourse Delivered Before The American Colonization Society, May 1880 – Scope and Meaning of Africa', in *The Original African Heritage Study Bible* (Nashville: The James C. Winston Publishing Co., 1993), pp. 109–21.

14 Blyden, 'Africa's Service to the World', pp. 109–21.

15 Blyden, 'Africa's Service to the World', p. 109.

16 See Robert Beckford, *Dread and Pentecostal: A Political Theology for the Black Church in Britain* (London: SPCK, 2000), pp. 83–6.

17 See Anthony G. Reddie, *Dramatizing Theologies: A Participative Approach to Black God-Talk* (London: Equinox, 2006), pp. 160–78.

18 Robert Beckford, *God and the Gangs* (London: DLT, 2004), p. 75.

19 See Gayraud S. Wilmore, *Black Religion and Black Radicalism* (Maryknoll: Orbis, 1983), pp. 103–86.

20 See Anthony B. Pinn, *Terror and Triumph* (Minneapolis: Fortress Press, 2003).

21 James W. Perkinson, *White Theology: Outing Supremacy in Modernity* (New York: Palgrave Macmillan, 2005), pp. 51–86.

22 To understand Robert Beckford's canon, see Michael N. Jagessar and Anthony G. Reddie (eds), *Black Theology in Britain: A Reader* (London: Equinox, 2007), pp. 81–108.

23 See Reddie, *Nobodies to Somebodies*, pp. 66–73.

24 See Anthony B. Pinn and Dwight N. Hopkins (eds), *Loving the Body: Black Religious Studies and the Erotic* (New York: Palgrave, 2005).

25 See Kelly Brown Douglas, *What's Faith Got to Do with It?* (Maryknoll: Orbis, 2005).

26 See James H. Cone, *A Black Theology of Liberation* (New York: Orbis, 1990), p. 121.

27 See Cone, *A Black Theology of Liberation.*

28 See Cone, *A Black Theology of Liberation*, p. 117.

29 See <http://www.creflodollarministries.org/> for further details of his ministry.

30 See <http://www.kicc.org.uk/> for further details of his ministry.

31 See Robert Beckford, 'Theology in the Age of Crack: Crack Age, Prosperity Doctrine and "Being There"', *Black Theology in Britain: A Journal of Contextual Praxis* (Vol. 4, No. 1, 2001), pp. 9–24.

32 This lies at the heart of what I am now terming a participative approach to Black theology. See Anthony G. Reddie, *Acting in Solidarity: Reflections in Critical Christianity* (London: DLT, 2005) and *Dramatizing Theologies.*

33 See 'The Parable of the Good Punk Rocker' in Paul Burbridge and Murray Watts, *Time To Act: Sketches and Guidelines for Biblical Drama* (London: Hodder & Stoughton, 1979), pp. 78–80.

34 Burbridge and Watts, *Time To Act.*

35 Footnotes on Luke 10.27–39 in *The Original African Heritage Study Bible*, p. 1499.

36 I address issues of my own development and social progress and mobility in a previous piece of work. See Anthony G. Reddie, *Black Theology in Transatlantic Dialogue* (New York: Palgrave Macmillan, 2006), pp. 8–15.

37 See Theodore W. Jennings Jr., *Good News to the Poor: John Wesley's Evangelical Economics* (Nashville: Abingdon Press, 1990), pp. 47–69.

38 See Kenneth Leech, *Through Our Long Exile* (London: DLT, 2001).

39 Reddie, *Dramatizing Theologies*, pp. 103–5.

40 Robert Hood's landmark text of the early 1990s addresses this issue head on. See Robert E. Hood, *Must God Remain Greek?: Afro-Cultures and God Talk* (Minneapolis: Fortress Press, 1990).

2 Proverbial wisdom

1 Robert Beckford has charted the mutating forms of racism since the era of slavery and the many ways in which African Caribbean people have resisted this constant scourge in their lives. See Robert Beckford, *Dread and Pentecostal* (London: SPCK, 2000), pp. 67–130.

2 See Chapter 3, 'Self-discovery: deconstructing Whiteness?'

3 See Anthony G. Reddie, *Nobodies to Somebodies: A Practical Theology for Education and Liberation* (Peterborough: Epworth Press, 2003), pp. 152–74.

4 See also Anthony G. Reddie, *Growing into Hope: Christian Education in Multi-Ethnic Churches – in Two Volumes. Vol. 1 Believing and Expecting* (Peterborough: Methodist Publishing House, 1998) and *Vol. 2 Liberation and Change* (Peterborough: Methodist Publishing House, 1998).

5 Lawrence N. Jones, 'Hope for Mankind: Insights from Black Religious History in the United States', *Journal of Religious Thought* (Vol. 34, No. 2, Fall–Winter, 1978), p. 59.

6 See Anthony G. Reddie, *Dramatizing Theologies: A Participative Approach to Black God-Talk* (London: Equinox, 2006), p. 188.

7 Robert Beckford, *God and the Gangs* (London: DLT, 2004), pp. 31–2.

8 Beckford, *God and the Gangs*, pp. 17–19.

9 For aspects of this African retentive form of spiritual wisdom, see Marvia E. Lawes, 'A Historical Evaluation of Jamaica Baptists: A Spirituality of

Resistance', *Black Theology: An International Journal* (Vol. 6, No. 3, 2008), pp. 366–92.

10 The Caribbean African American woman theologian Dianne Stewart explores this interchange between the 'present' and the 'past' in her highly influential work on the Jamaican/Caribbean religious identity since the era of slavery. See Dianne M. Stewart, *Three Eyes for the Journey: African Dimensions of the Jamaican Religious Experience* (New York: Oxford University Press, 2005).

11 See Anthony B. Pinn, *Terror and Triumph: The Nature of Black Religion* (Minneapolis: Fortress Press, 2003), pp. 81–156.

12 See Pinn, *Terror and Triumph*, 2003.

13 See Reddie, *Nobodies to Somebodies*, pp. 14–20.

14 See Mukti Barton, *Rejection, Resistance and Resurrection* (London: DLT, 2005) for perhaps the best scholarly, first-hand account of Black and Asian people's experience of dealing with racism in the Church of England.

15 See Reddie, *Growing into Hope (Vol. 2): Liberation and Change*, pp. 33–7.

16 See Randall C. Bailey, 'Race, Racism and Biblical Narratives', in Cain Hope Felder (ed.), *Stony the Road We Trod: African American Biblical Interpretation* (Minneapolis: Fortress Press, 1991), pp. 165–84.

17 The relationship between the two schemes of epistemologies (sources and frameworks for knowledge and truth) – Hebrew/Old Testament and African (some will argue that the two are essentially the same things) – is dealt with in great detail by Jamaican Woman theologian Marjorie Lewis. See Marjorie A. Lewis, 'Towards A Systematic Spirituality for Black British Women', (unpublished PhD thesis, the University of Birmingham, 2007).

18 See Charles E. Melchert, *Wise Teaching: Biblical Wisdom and Educational Ministry* (Harrisburg: Trinity Press International, 1998).

19 See Jack Daniel and Geneva Smitherman-Donaldson, 'How I Got Over: Communication Dynamics in the Black Community', *Quarterly Journal of Speech*, No. 62, February 1976, p. 35.

20 See David Day, 'Apples of Gold: The Role of Proverbial Wisdom in Christian Education', in Jeff Astley and David Day (eds), *The Contours of Christian Education* (Great Wakering: McCrimmons, 1992), pp. 162–76.

21 Further details on the theology and learning of 'Sophia' can be found in Melchert, *Wise Teaching*.

22 See Diane Watt, 'Traditional Religious Practices amongst African Caribbean Mother and Community Othermothers', *Black Theology: An International Journal* (Vol. 2, No. 2, July 2004), pp. 195–212.

23 This issue is dealt with in one of my earlier books. See Anthony G. Reddie, *Faith, Stories and the Experience of Black Elders* (London: Jessica Kingsley, 2001).

24 Melchert, *Wise Teaching*, pp. 205–71.

25 Melchert, *Wise Teaching*, pp. 205–71.
26 See Ella P. Mitchell, 'Oral Tradition: The Legacy of Faith for the Black Church', *Religious Education* (18.1, 1986), pp. 93–113.
27 For further reflections on Martin Luther King's notion of the 'beloved community', see Lewis V. Baldwin, *Towards the Beloved Community* (Cleveland: Pilgrim Press, 1995).
28 See Paulo Freire, *A Pedagogy of Hope* (New York: Continuum, 1994).
29 Biblical scholar William Hertzog says something to this effect in his classic text from the mid-1990s. See William Hertzog II, *The Parables as Subversive Speech: Jesus as Pedagogue of the Oppressed* (Louisville: John Knox Westminster Press, 1994).
30 Indian New Testament scholar David Joy argues that Jesus' message attracted a significant following from the 'subalterns' – the marginalized outsiders of his day. The presence of these people can be seen in the references to the crowd in Mark's Gospel account. See C. I. David Joy, *Mark and its Subalterns: A Hermeneutical Paradigm for a Postcolonial Context* (London: Equinox, 2008).
31 See Bhikhu Parekh, *Rethinking Multiculturalism: Cultural Diversity and Political Theory* (Basingstoke: Macmillan, 2000).
32 See the dramatic sketch 'Grasping the Chaos' in Anthony G. Reddie, *Acting in Solidarity: Reflections in Critical Christianity* (London: DLT, 2005), pp. 127–35.

3 Self-discovery

1 See Dwight N. Hopkins, *Being Human: Race, Culture and Religion* (Minneapolis: Fortress Press, 2005).
2 For further information on the links between Black people of African Caribbean descent and White British people who share surnames and ancestral links, see Robert Beckford, *God of the Rahtid* (London: DLT, 2003), pp. 62–97. For more general and accessible information on the transatlantic slave, see Richard S. Reddie, *Abolition* (Oxford: Lion Books, 2008).
3 Paul Gilroy remains the main articulator of this complex dynamic of 'race' culture and nationality. See his *'There Ain't No Black in The Union Jack': The Cultural Politics of Race and Nation* (London: Hutchinson, 1987) and *The Black Atlantic: modernity and double consciousness* (London: Verso, 1993).
4 See James Cone's landmark trilogy of books, *Black Theology and Black Power* (Maryknoll: Orbis, 1997, first published 1969), *A Black Theology of Liberation* (Maryknoll: Orbis, 1990, first published 1970) and *God of the Oppressed* (Maryknoll: Orbis, 1997, first published 1975). See also his *Martin, Malcolm and America: A Dream or a Nightmare?* (Maryknoll: Orbis, 1992).

5 Feminist scholars like Mary Daly and Daphne Hampson have critiqued Christianity for its androcentric (male-centred) and patriarchal (normative male power) frameworks that have led directly to the lesser treatment of women within the Church and beyond it. See Mary Daly, *Beyond God the Father* (London: The Women's Press, 1986). See also Daphne Hampson, *After Christianity* (London: SCM Press, 1996).

6 See Harry H. Singleton III, *Black Theology and Ideology: Deideological Dimensions in the Theology of James H. Cone* (Collegeville: Liturgical Press, 2002) and Lewin Williams, *Caribbean Theology* (New York: Peter Laing, 1994).

7 See Cornel West, *Prophecy Deliverance!: An Afro-American Revolutionary Christianity* (Philadelphia: Westminster Press, 1982).

8 See *Jesus is Dread: Black Theology and Black Culture in Britain* (London: DLT, 1998). For a helpful overarching treatment on the differing methodological paradigms for undertaking Black theology, see Frederick L. Ware, *Methodologies of Black Theology* (Cleveland: Pilgrim Press, 2002). See also Robert Beckford, *Jesus is Dread* and *Dread and Pentecostalism* (London: SPCK, 2000).

9 See Frederick L. Ware, *Methodologies of Black Theology* (Cleveland: Pilgrim Press, 2002), pp. 100–1.

10 See Ware, *Methodologies of Black Theology*, pp. 28–65.

11 As the majority of Black people in Britain live in urban conurbations, the contexts where White people meet us are often in urban situations and the institutions and formal and informal networks that exist there. For further reflections on this, see Anthony G. Reddie, 'Exploring the Workings of Black Theology in Britain: Issues of Theological Method and Epistemological Construction', *Black Theology: An International Journal* (Vol. 7, No. 1, 2009), pp. 64–85.

12 See James W. Perkinson, *White Theology: Outing Supremacy in Modernity* (New York: Palgrave Macmillan, 2004) and *Shamanism, Racism and Hip Hop Culture: Essays on White Supremacy and Black Subversion* (New York: Palgrave Macmillan, 2005). See also Laurie M. Cassidy and Alex Mikulich (eds), *Interrupting White Privilege: Catholic Theologians Break the Silence* (Maryknoll: Orbis, 2007).

13 See also Cassidy and Mikulich (eds), *Interrupting White Privilege.*

14 See Jennifer Harvey, *Whiteness and Morality: Pursuing Racial Justice Through Reparations and Sovereignty* (New York: Palgrave Macmillan, 2007).

15 See Thandeka, *Learning to be White: Money, Race and God in America* (New York and London: Continuum, 2000).

16 Vron Ware and Les Back (eds), *Out of Whiteness: Color, Politics and Culture* (Chicago and London: University of Chicago Press, 2002).

17 Elsewhere, I argue that the foundational creation of modernity represents the definitional change that occurred among enslaved Africans who

were suddenly defined as 'Negroes'. See Anthony G. Reddie, 'Black Ecclesiologies', in Gerard Mannion and Lewis S. Mudge (eds), *The Routledge Companion to the Christian Church* (New York and London: Routledge, 2008), pp. 443–60. See also Anthony B. Pinn, *Terror and Triumph* (Minneapolis: Fortress Press, 2003), pp. 1–23.

18 James Cone describes White supremacy as the 'great sin' of modernity. See James H. Cone, 'Theology's Great Sin: Silence in the Face of White Supremacy', *Black Theology: An International Journal* (Vol. 2, No. 2, July 2004), pp. 139–52.

19 This issue is addressed in one of my previous books. See Anthony G. Reddie, *Black Theology in Transatlantic Dialogue* (New York: Palgrave Macmillan, 2006), pp. 86 and 87.

20 In terms of Black theology in Britain both Robert Beckford and Anthony Reddie have explored notions of White privilege in their work. See Robert Beckford, *God and the Gangs* (London: DLT, 2005), pp. 72–81. See also Anthony G. Reddie *Dramatizing Theologies: A Participative Approach to Black God-Talk* (London: Equinox, 2006), pp. 46–51.

4 Reading the Bible with Black theology

1 I have addressed the balance in terms of the location of authority between the concerns of the author of the text (in terms of the socio-cultural, economic and political background), the normative readings of what occurs within the text itself and the Liberationist concerns of Black people from in front of the text (as the reader) in a previous piece of work. See Anthony G. Reddie, *Working Against the Grain: Re-imaging Black Theology in the 21st Century* (London: Equinox, 2008), pp. 49–74.

2 For a number of excellent texts that offer historical perspectives on this development, see Cain Hope Felder (ed.), *The Original African Heritage Study Bible* (Nashville: The James C. Winston Publishing Co., 1993), Vincent L. Wimbush, *The Bible and African Americans: A Brief History* (Minneapolis: Fortress Press, 2003), Vincent L. Wimbush (ed.), *African Americans and the Bible: Sacred Texts and Social Textures* (New York and London: Continuum, 2000), Michael Joseph Brown, *The Blackening of the Bible: The Aims of African American Biblical Scholarship* (Harrisburg: Trinity Press International, 2004), Allen Dwight Callahan, *The Talking Book: African Americans and the Bible* (New Haven: Yale University Press, 2006), Brian K. Blount (ed.), *True to Our Native Land: An African American New Testament Commentary* (Minneapolis: Fortress Press, 2007) and Curtiss Paul DeYoung, Wilda C. Gafney, Leticia A. Guardiola-Saenz, George E. Tinker and Frank M. Yamada (eds), *The Peoples' Bible* (Minneapolis: Fortress Press, 2008).

3 See Anthony G. Reddie, *Dramatizing Theologies: A Participative Approach to Black God-Talk* (London: Equinox, 2006), pp. 44–6. See also Dwight

N. Hopkins, *Introducing Black Theology of Liberation* (Maryknoll: Orbis, 1999), pp. 23–38.

4 Among Cain Hope Felder's key works are: Cain Hope Felder (ed.), *The Original African Heritage Study Bible* (Nashville: The James C. Winston Publishing Co., 1993); Cain Hope Felder, *Troubling Biblical Waters* (Maryknoll: Orbis, 1989) and Cain Hope Felder (ed.), *Stony the Road We Trod: African American Biblical Interpretation* (Minneapolis: Augsburg/ Fortress Press, 1991).

5 Among Randall C. Bailey's key works are: Randall C. Bailey and Jacquelyn Grant (eds), *The Recovery of Black Presence: An Interdisciplinary Exploration* (Nashville: Abingdon, 1995) and Randall C. Bailey (ed.), *Yet With A Steady Beat: Contemporary U.S. Afrocentric Biblical Interpretation* (Atlanta: Society For Biblical Literature, 2003).

6 See Michael Joseph Brown, *The Blackening of the Bible: The Aims of African American Biblical Scholarship* (Harrisburg: Trinity Press International, 2004), pp. 1–23.

7 Brown, *The Blackening of the Bible*, p. 2.

8 See Ron Ramdin, *Reimaging Britain* (London: Pluto Press, 1999), pp. 5–10.

9 See Stephen R. Haynes, *Noah's Curse: The Biblical Justification of Slavery* (Oxford and New York: Oxford University Press, 2002). See also Sylvester A. Johnson, *The Myth of Ham in Nineteenth-Century American Christianity* (New York: Palgrave Macmillan, 2004).

10 See Kelly Brown Douglas, *What's Faith Got to Do with It?: Black Bodies/ Christian Souls* (New York: Orbis, 2005).

11 The chief proponent of the discourse arguing for the economic underpinning of the transatlantic slave trade (rather than one based primarily on racialized ideology) is Eric Williams. See Eric Williams, *Capitalism and Slavery* (London: Andre Deutsch, 1990). While not seeking to rework Williams' argument in any substantive way, it is worth acknowledging the more recent scholarship of African American Black theologian Dwight N. Hopkins, who locates contemporary models of Black exploitation, and the disenfranchisement of other people of colour in the so-called Third World, within a wider framework of globalized monopoly capitalism. See Dwight N. Hopkins, *Head and Heart* (New York: Palgrave Macmillan, 2002), pp. 127–52.

12 African American Biblical scholar Theodore Burgh offers an important, critical assessment of the relationship between Black Biblical interpretation and archaeology in a comparatively recent piece of work. See Theodore W. Burgh, 'Black Biblical Interpretation and Near Eastern Archaeology', *Black Theology: An International Journal* (Vol. 4, No. 2, 2006), pp. 138–50.

13 Cain Hope Felder and Randall Bailey address the ways in which Black presence in the Bible has been hidden or overlooked by predominantly

White Euro-American Biblical scholars. See Cain Hope Felder (ed.), *The Original African Heritage Study Bible*, p. 1377. See also Randall C. Bailey, 'Beyond Identification: The Use of Africans in Old Testament Poetry and Narratives', in Felder (ed.), *Stony the Road We Trod*, pp. 127–45. See also Randall C. Bailey, '"Is That Any Name for a Nice Hebrew Boy?"' in Bailey and Grant (eds), *The Recovery of Black Presence*, pp. 25–36.

14 I am here referring to Felder (ed.), *Stony the Road We Trod.*

15 Anthony G. Reddie, *Black Theology in Transatlantic Dialogue* (New York: Palgrave Macmillan, 2006), p. 133.

16 Michael N. Jagessar and Anthony G. Reddie (eds), *Black Theology in Britain: A Reader* (London: Equinox, 2007), p. 1.

17 See James H. Cone, *Black Theology and Black Power* (Maryknoll: Orbis, 1997, first published in 1969).

18 James H. Cone, *A Black Theology of Liberation* (Maryknoll: Orbis, 1990, first published in 1970).

19 James H. Cone, *God of the Oppressed* (Maryknoll: Orbis, 1997, first published in 1975).

20 See Naim S. Ateek, 'A Palestinian Perspective: Biblical Perspectives on the Land', in R. S. Sugirtharajah (ed.), *Voices from the Margin: Interpreting the Bible in the Third World* (London and New York: SPCK and Orbis, 1997), pp. 267–76. See also Robert Allen Warrior, 'A Native American Perspective: Canaanites, Cowboys, and Indians', in Sugirtharajah (ed.), *Voices from the Margin*, pp. 277–85.

21 See Warrior, 'A Native American Perspective', pp. 277–85.

22 This theme is addressed by the African American Black theologian Josiah Young. See Josiah U. Young III, 'Distinguishing Sterility from Fecundity in the Wesleyan Tradition', in Jorg Rieger and John J. Vincent (eds), *Methodist and Radical: Rejuvenating a Tradition* (Nashville: Abingdon Press, 2003), pp. 67–76.

23 I am using 'lost' and 'loss' in the broadest sense to mean anyone who is temporarily or permanently separated from us.

24 See Felder (ed.), *The Original Africa Heritage Study Bible.*

25 See Anthony B. Pinn and Dwight N. Hopkins (eds), *Loving the Body: Black Religious Studies and the Erotic* (New York: Palgrave Macmillan, 2004).

26 I use the term 'official' pictures or Gospels of Jesus because, as many scholars have shown, there are other accounts of Jesus' life that were written at the time of the canonical versions, but not accepted as part of the official canon. See R. S. Sugirtharajah, *Troublesome Texts: The Bible in Colonial and Contemporary Culture* (Sheffield: Sheffield Phoenix Press, 2008), pp. 52–5.

27 See James H. Cone, *God of the Oppressed* (New York: Seabury Press, 1975).

28 See Jacquelyn Grant, *White Women's Christ and Black Women's Jesus* (Atlanta: Scholar's Press, 1989).

29 William R. Jones, *Is God a White Racist?: A Preamble to Black Theology* (Boston: Beacon Press, 1998, first published in 1973).
30 Anthony B. Pinn, *Why, Lord?: Sin and Suffering in Black Theology* (New York: Continuum, 1995).
31 See Dwight N. Hopkins, *Down, Up and Over: Slave Religion and Black Theology* (Minneapolis: Fortress Press, 2000). See also Anthony B. Pinn, *Terror and Triumph: The Nature of Black Religion* (Minneapolis: Fortress Press, 2003).
32 Although slavery began and ended in varying parts of the world at different times, it is estimated that Britain was the main economic beneficiary of the transatlantic slave trade and her active involvement dates back to approximately 1562. The last major nation to end the chattel enslavement of Black Africans was Brazil in 1888. See Richard S. Reddie, *Abolition: The Struggle to Abolish Slavery in the British Colonies* (Oxford: Lion Books, 2007).
33 See Reddie, *Working Against the Grain*, pp. 137–56.
34 See Delores Williams, *Sisters in the Wilderness: The Challenge of Womanist God Talk* (Maryknoll: Orbis, 1993).

5 Preaching the Bible

1 For an excellent critique of global capitalism from a Christian Liberationist perspective, see Wilfe Wilde, *Crossing the River of Fire: Mark's Gospel and Global Capitalism* (Peterborough: Epworth Press, 2006).
2 This activity began as an experiential exercise but has since been developed into a participative sermon for use in worship. The development and transition of the exercise accords with the movement in my participative approach to preaching detailed in a previous piece of work. See Anthony G. Reddie, 'An Interactive Odyssey', in Geoffrey Stevenson, *Pulpit Journeys* (London: DLT, 2006), pp. 149–66.
3 Perhaps the most significant theological analysis of the slave trade from a Black Liberationist perspective is to be found in *Black Theology: An International Journal* (Vol. 5, No. 2, 2007).
4 See Richard S. Reddie, *Abolition: The Struggle to Abolish Slavery in the British Colonies* (Oxford: Lion Books, 2007).
5 See Robert Beckford, *Empire Pays Back* (15 August 2005, Channel 4).
6 William K. Hertzog II, *Jesus, Justice and the Reign of God: A Ministry of Liberation* (Louisville: Westminster John Knox Press, 2000).
7 Mark Lewis Taylor, *The Executed God: The Way of the Cross in Lockdown America* (Minneapolis: Fortress Press, 2001).
8 See David C. I. Joy, *Mark and its Subalterns: A Hermeneutical Paradigm for a Postcolonial Context* (London: Equinox, 2008).
9 Robert Beckford, *God of the Rahtid* (London: DLT, 2001), p. 12.
10 See Gustavo Gutiérrez, *A Theology of Liberation* (London: SCM Press, 1988).

6 Preaching theology

1 James H. Cone, *Black Theology and Black Power* (Maryknoll: Orbis, 2003), p. 120.

2 See James H. Cone, *God of the Oppressed* (New York: Seabury Press, 1975), pp. 138–62.

3 See James D. Holway (ed.), *Sermons on Several Occasions by the Reverend John Wesley* (Ilkeston: Moorley's, 1996). This sermon is a Black theology reinterpretation of John Wesley's 38th sermon on original sin.

4 See Anthony G. Reddie, 'Original Sin: No. 38', in Angela Shier-Jones and Kimberly D. Reisman (eds), *44 Sermons to Serve the Present Age* (Peterborough: Epworth Press, 2007), pp. 232–41. Reproduced by permission.

5 The basic methodological and theological underpinning to my preaching ministry can be found in Anthony G. Reddie, 'An Interactive Odyssey', in Geoffrey Stevenson (ed.), *Pulpit Journeys* (London: DLT, 2006), pp. 149–65. In this essay I stress that my preaching is built upon a participative mode of engagement in which I use experiential exercises and drama as ways of creating a relationship between the contingency of the contemporary context and the historicity of the biblical text. This participative style is also informed by the theological framework of improvisation found within jazz music. For further details, see Anthony G. Reddie, *Black Theology in Transatlantic Dialogue* (New York: Palgrave Macmillan, 2006), pp. 167–99.

6 See note 4 above.

7 See Darnell Moore's important contribution to Black theology where he critiques the notion of sin as it is applied disproportionately to Black people in same-gender loving relationships in many African American Churches. See Darnell L. Moore, 'Guilty of Sin: African American Denominational Churches and Exclusion of SGL Sisters and Brothers', *Black Theology: An International Journal* (Vol. 6, No. 1, 2008), pp. 83–97.

8 This question of how theology is shaped by the experience of largely poor, marginalized and oppressed Black women is addressed by a number of African American Womanist theologians in a comparatively recent publication. See Stacey M. Floyd-Thomas (ed.), *Deeper Shades of Purple: Womanism in Religion and Society* (New York and London: New York University Press, 2006).

9 See Jacquelyn Grant, *White Women's Christ and Black Women's Jesus* (Atlanta: Scholar's Press, 1989), pp. 63–90.

Afterword

1 See Robert E. Hood, *Begrimed and Black: Christian Traditions on Blacks and Blackness* (Minneapolis: Fortress Press, 1994), pp. 23–43.

2 See Robert E. Hood, *Begrimed and Black*, pp. 23–43.

3 Robert Beckford, *Dread and Pentecostal* (London: SPCK, 2000), pp. 95–130.

4 See Emmanuel C. Eze, *'Race' and the Enlightenment* (Oxford: Blackwell, 1997).

5 See James W. Perkinson, *White Theology* (New York: Palgrave, 2004), pp. 154–84.

6 Dwight N. Hopkins, *Being Human: 'Race' Culture and Religion* (Minneapolis: Fortress Press, 2005), pp. 144–60.

7 It is important to make the point that not all White Christians are guilty of this behaviour. Examples of alternative practices can be found. See Kenneth Leech, *Through Our Long Exile* (London: DLT, 2001); Kenneth Leech, *Doing Theology in Altab Park* (London: DLT, 2005), Kenneth Leech, *Race: Changing Society and the Churches* (London: SPCK, 2005), Kenneth Leech, *Struggle in Babylon: Racism in the Cities and Churches of Britain* (London: Sheldon Press, 1988). See also David Haslam, *Race for the Millennium: The Challenge to Church and Society* (London: Churches Commission for Racial Justice (CCRJ): 1996), John L. Wilkinson, *Church in Black and White* (Edinburgh: Saint Andrews Press, 1990) and Timothy J. Gorringe, *Furthering Humanity: A Theology of Culture* (Farnham: Ashgate, 2004).

8 See Michael N. Jagessar and Anthony G. Reddie (eds) *Black Theology in Britain: A Reader* (London: Routledge, 2007), pp. 39–46.

9 I have addressed this issue on pp. 37–52 of this book.

10 Prior to becoming Prime Minister, Boris Johnson was a committed defender of British colonialism and empire. I cannot see how these reported views are compatible with even the most basic of commitments to Black Lives Matter. See <https://independent.co.uk/news/uk/politics/boris-johnson-colonialism-africa-british-empire-slavery-a9564541.html?fbclid=IwAR08hl76GjxOvbWnzMLmSBhjq7YRwwvj80psPcK9_xEo-4ExwcJl06-mzBEA> (accessed 14 June 2020).

11 See the brilliant article by James Cone, the architect of Black theology. James H. Cone 'Theology's Great Sin: Silence in the Face of White Supremacy', *Black Theology: An International Journal* (Vol. 2, No.2, July 2004), pp. 139–52.

12 See the following for details of this service, which was only discontinued in 2017 <https://bristolpost.co.uk/news/bristol-news/bristol-church-refuses-host-most-782798> (accessed 14 June 2020).

13 See William R. Hertzog II, *Jesus, Justice and the Reign of God* (Louisville: Westminster John Knox Press, 1999).

14 New International Financial and Economic Architecture (NIFEA) is a panel of experts in theology and economics convened by the World Council of Churches, World Communion of Reformed Churches, Council for World Mission and the Lutheran World Federation in New York from 21 to 22 April 2018. It underlined two critical consequences of the current financial and economic system: the widening wealth

gap and climate change. For further details of this ongoing work, see: <https://oikoumene.org/en/resources/documents/wcc-programmes/concept-note-of-nifea-workshop-on-just-taxation-and-reparations-16-20-march-2019> (accessed 14 June 2020).

15 I am indebted to my friend and former CWM colleague, the Revd Dr Peter Cruchley for this pithy and insightful observation.

16 I must commend the prophetic work of the Council for World Mission (formerly the London Missionary Society – LMS) that has committed itself to a process of examining its own involvement in the nefarious slave trade and its wider collusion with empire and colonialism. This work on the legacies of slavery is committed to offering reparations to the descendants of enslaved Africans, seeking to go beyond the rhetoric of apology and sorry. See the following for more on this work: <https://cwmission.org/what-we-do/cutting-edge-mission-initiatives/legacies-of-slavery> (accessed 14 June 2020).

Index